Experimental embroidery

Experimental embroidery

Edith John

Charles T Branford Co
Newton Centre, Mass 02159

Copyright Edith John 1976
First published in the USA 1976

ISBN 0-8231-4255-8

Library of Congress Cataloging Data
John, Edith
Experimental Embroidery
1 Embroidery. I Title
TT770.J578   746.4'4   75-9521
ISBN 0-8231-4255-8

Printed in Great Britain
for the publishers
Charles T Branford Company
28 Union Street
Newton Centre, Massachusetts

Contents

Acknowledgment   6

Introduction   7

1   New frames and their uses   9

2   Unusual supports for embroidery   24

3   Manipulating fabrics   39

4   Inspiration from unusual objects   66

5   Manipulating stitches   81

6   Soft and hard sculpture   95

Conclusion   113

Further reading   114

Suppliers   115

Index   118

Acknowledgment

It is always a pleasure to acknowledge the help and advice which is so willingly given to an author by numerous friends and colleagues. First and foremost I must thank Mr and Mrs Platt for reading the script and for typing it for me, two really boring tasks which are always undertaken with a smile.

Mr Byrne has once again produced most of the excellent photographs in his usual professional manner. I am deeply indebted to him for his work.

It is impossible to say how grateful I am to those who have most generously allowed me to publish their original ideas and use photographs of their work. Their contribution to this book is a large one.

Last but not least my thanks must be given to the dozens of people, who all unwittingly have provided, by chance remarks, inspiration for further experiments.

Doncaster 1976   E J

This book is dedicated to those who suffer from that strange curiosity which the Greeks held to be the beginning of wisdom and the seed of knowledge.

Introduction

The physicist J Robert Oppenheimer said of the structure of life and of the universe 'It is not arranged in a line, nor a square, nor a circle, but with a wonderful randomness suggestive of unending growth and improvisation'. What a reassuring sentence that is to embroiderers who long to be free to follow their own lines of thought, and who (even in these days when one can say with some truth that needle-craft has burst beyond the narrow confines of yesterday), are all too frequently thwarted by friends and teachers who oppose originality. At this point a word of warning is necessary. No one can successfully experiment unless one understands with what one is experimenting. It follows, therefore, that a sound knowledge of traditional methods of embroidery and stitches is essential before one begins to overthrow all restrictions. Experimenting for experiment's sake is most stimulating, but the moment of truth can be a grim one if the experiment, though dazzling to the eye and satisfying to the inventor, is never going to lead to any-thing worthwhile.

Those who have a practical turn of mind, apart from the artists who realize that art serves no useful purpose, deserve some consideration. After all, it scarcely needs stressing that artists are in the minority. A large amount of creative work is done for domestic and ecclesiastical purposes, and it is obvious that it must be reasonably durable and capable of being cleaned. There is a great deal of talk today about disposable embroidery, and I do agree that some work should be considered as such, but that which is supposed to be wearable should surely last for a season, and since ecclesiastical embroidery is so expensive it is only reason-able to expect it to have a life of at least a decade. We must also consider posterity. Think how much our culture would have suffered if all the embroideries which were created hundreds of years ago had been disposed of. Is it then a vicious circle? Must creative and experimental work be regarded as an end in themselves? Of course not. It is first necessary to experiment freely, without the need to con-sider either suitability for purpose or practical matters like cleaning, and then, after a valuable new idea has been ex-plored fully, to adapt it for all kinds of practical purposes.

This then is my reason, and excuse if one is needed, for writing a book about experimental embroidery, much of which will appear to be highly impractical and probably useless. However, many practical uses for the experiments described have already been found, and if readers will only indulge in one of those 'brilliant flashes of silence' so beloved by Macauley, I am sure they will be convinced of the value of creative work.

1 New frames and their uses

The mention of a frame in conjunction with embroidery seems to divide needlewomen neatly into two opposing groups; those who would not dream of using a frame for any purpose, and those who regard the frame as a third hand and a most valuable piece of equipment. The battle between these two groups is as keen as that which is often waged between the practical and the creative embroiderer. It is all a matter of taste, but I would hasten to add that some kinds of work really do need the support of a frame if good technique is to be achieved, and some stitches are very pleasant to work on fabric which is held over the fingers.

There is another way of looking at this problem of to frame or not to frame one's work. Begin at the end and think of the laborious and painstaking process of mounting finished panels, and the high cost of professional framing. Why not start by making a perfectly matching frame quite cheaply and mounting the background before executing a single stitch, thus saving cost and time, and giving oneself greater freedom to sew creatively? All that is required is a simple wooden frame which can be made easily at home with materials bought from a do-it-yourself shop. Some schools have their woodwork departments and have no problem, and the unhandy person will find that some picture framers or even joiner friends will produce neat frames if given the correct measurements and instructions. The frame should be made of smooth white wood, with mitred corners capable of withstanding some pressure. Avoid frames which have a piece of wood or metal across the corners to strengthen them as they are unsightly, and prevent the embroiderer making full use of the frame. Any thickness of wood may be used, and for preference a beginner should use either a square or oblong frame. Having obtained a frame, smooth it with emery paper if necessary, and for a really professional finish pad it with strips of foam on the top and both sides, but not on the back. Use *copydex* (or a strong white glue) sparingly and do not press the foam hard, otherwise dents will appear and they cannot be removed. To calculate the amount of fabric which will be needed first measure firmly but not tightly round the frame and add 13 mm ($\frac{1}{2}$ in.) to this measurement. This gives the width of the four pieces which will be needed to cover the sides of the frame. To obtain the length measure the sides and add 25 mm (1 in.). Do not allow more as extra fabric causes difficulties and it will have to be cut off sooner or later. Remember to cut on the straight of the fabric, and if it is spotted, striped or patterned in any way do consider how it will lie on the frame. The piece of fabric required for the background should be as large as the outer dimensions of the frame plus 13 mm ($\frac{1}{2}$ in.) turning all round. Thus a frame which is 305 mm (12 in.) square needs a piece of fabric 381 mm (13 in.) square.

To cover the frame

Place one strip of fabric face downwards on a table, and put one edge of the frame face downwards upon it, leaving 13 mm ($\frac{1}{2}$ in.) of material at each end. Now paste the uppermost surface of the frame with *copydex*, beginning and ending 38 mm ($1\frac{1}{2}$ in.) from the inner corners (*1*).

Fold the fabric over the frame from the outside to the inside and press it firmly into position, smoothing it from the centre outwards, to ensure a good fit (*2*). Repeat on the remaining three sides, by which time the first side will be dry and ready for the next step. Paste the same area as before, draw the inner edge of the cloth firmly over to the outside of the frame and press it into position (*3*).

Complete the other sides and turn the frame right way up. Push one of the loose ends backwards and press the other into the corner so that it fits like a cuff (*4*). From the inside of the frame cut 13 mm ($\frac{1}{2}$ in.) from the corner to the top of the wood (*5*).

Press the uncut fabric over the mitre of the frame and cut it right across to the outer edge, leaving 13 mm ($\frac{1}{2}$ in.) turning on the mitre (*6*).

Fold in all the turnings and complete the pasting on the wrong side. **Do not paste anywhere else.** Repeat on the seven remaining loose ends, then with a matching or invisible thread ladder stitch the folded edges together, pulling the thread firmly to close the seam (*7*).

Turn the frame face downwards. Press 13 mm ($\frac{1}{2}$ in.) turnings on the right side of the background fabric, place the right side upon the frame and pin one corner (*8*).

Pull the fabric tightly and place pins about 25 mm (1 in.) apart down two sides. If the fabric stretches it may be necessary to trim the other two sides before pinning them in position, as no raw edges should be seen on the right side of the work. When the pinning is complete the fabric should be tight and straight. Oversew the edge firmly to the frame, removing one pin at a time as the work progresses. If the background requires strengthening sew on loosely a piece of firm backing, or alternatively use iron-on

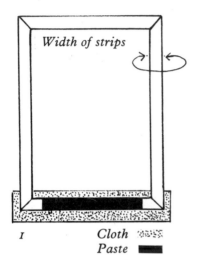

1   Cloth
       Paste

Width of strips

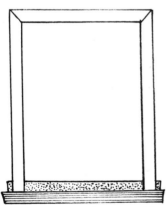

2 Fold cloth from outside, inwards

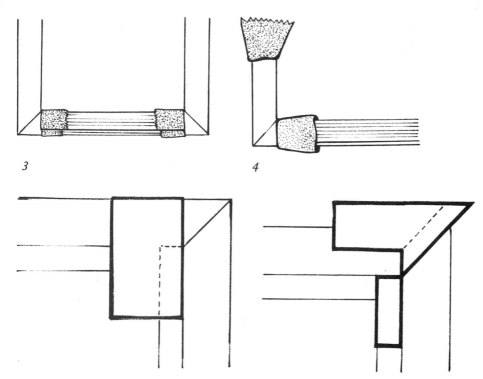

3

4

5   *Frame seen from inside.*
Cut on dotted lines

6   *Fold fabric on the mitre of*
the frame. Cut on dotted line

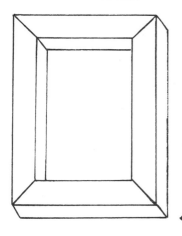

7

Begin to stitch at arrow and
continue right round the joins
and finish on the back

←

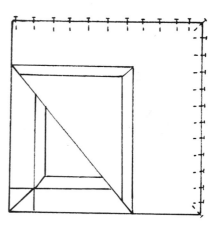

8   *Back of frame and cloth*

Ladder stitch
Pull stitches tight to close seam

Turn edge on right side of cloth,
and pin to the frame with the
wrong side uppermost

11

vilene. When the embroidery is finished protect the back of it by nailing a piece of strong card to the frame. Glass can be fixed over the front of the work with a narrow beading.

From this simple shape one should proceed to experiment with more unusual ones. Very deep, narrow frames with sloping inner edges are easy to cover, and in the diagrams other shapes which have proved successful are shown.

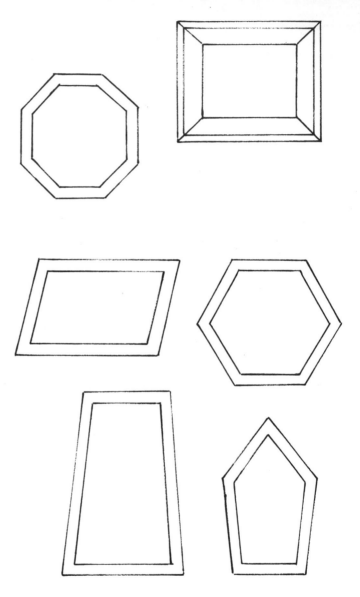

Frames of different shapes

Another type of frame which was devised to fit into a corner, especially at exhibitions, is also useful for free standing work. The construction of this right angled double frame is shown in diagram. An alternative way to make a right angled frame is to join two frames with a pair of hinges, and this can be done after the embroidery is finished. Several ideas for varying the arrangement of hinged frames is clearly shown in diagram (a).

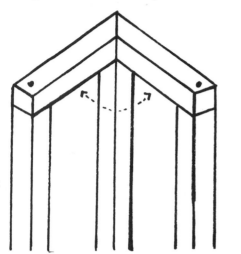

(a) Top of a right-angled frame

(b) Hinged right-angled frame

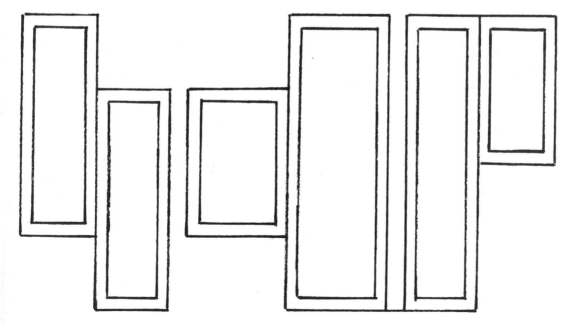

Hinged frames of various sizes

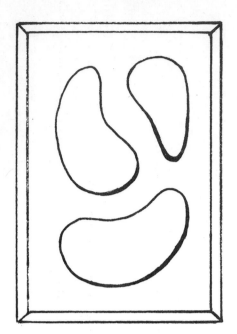

(a) Fabric stuck to back of card. Holes in card only

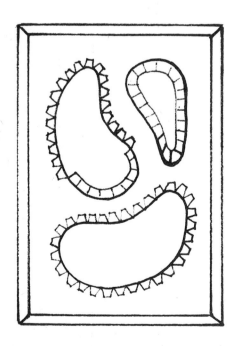

(b) Holes cut in cloth and 13 mm (½ in.) turnings glued back

From covering frames we proceed to the use of them. Some people are afraid to work upon a framed background and describe it as living dangerously, because the final result may be unsuccessful. This problem is easily overcome if the frame only is covered and the background worked separately. The finished piece should be mounted on card and nailed to the back of the frame. Neaten by sticking a piece of brown paper over the back of the work.

The more adventurous embroiderers fix their background to the frame and carry on with their work. In so doing the frame does more than edge a picture, it becomes an integral part of it, and there are many ways of achieving this end.

1 Many kinds of work, including appliqué, bead work and padded work look interesting if, on completion, a delicate tracery of needleweaving is worked right across the frame. See *Foreshore* page 17.

2 Depth and luminosity can be obtained by sewing straight, pleated or gathered chiffon across the top of finished work, from edge to edge of the frame. Torn or cut strips of coloured acetate give a similar effect. See *Underwater Ballet* by Olga Catterson page 18.

3 Strong nylon thread (we use fishing line) can be sewn in lines across the top of a frame and delicate stitchery and fine appliqué attached to them. Beads can be threaded on nylon too, and used either as a curtain over the work, or taken from the edge of the frame down into the background. See *Cumbrian Clouds* by Winifred Shield page 17.

4 Take stitchery or appliqué up from the background and over the edge of the frame. See *The Wave* page 19.

5 Some people like to make a Victorian Peep Show of their work. The background is richly embroidered, beads, sequins and gold being useful here, and then another piece of fabric, large enough to cover the frame plus generous turnings, is worked separately. On this spare piece, several fairly large spaces well away from the edge, are left unworked. When this piece is complete it is mounted on card as shown in the diagram, and then sewn to the top of the frame. *Method:*

Mark the spaces on a piece of strong card which is exactly the size of the frame, and cut them out. Stretch the embroidered fabric over this card and stick the edges to the back of it. Cut the holes out of the fabric leaving generous turnings. Snip, turn the card over and stick the turnings on the wrong side.

6 A much daintier effect is obtained if iron-on *vilene* is used instead of the card mentioned above. The turnings of many fabrics cannot be glued successfully to *vilene*, so the turnings are machined in a decorative manner. See *Holes*

Finnish needleweaving

by Joan Cooke page 21. A practical use for this method is obvious. It makes attractive modern cut work for dresses and lampshades. The turnings should be machined for a really practical result. To turn this into decoupé, tack the turnings round the holes in the *vilene*, and then tack a piece of fabric of contrasting colour behind the holes and machine as before.

7   For a firmer but still light effect use *parbond*, which can be ironed on the fabric after the holes have been cut out of it. This is particularly good for lampshades, as the *parbond* can be moulded to fit any shape. There is no need to leave turnings on fine fabrics.

8   Yet another method is to embroider the background, then to cut cardboard shapes and cover them with embroidered fabric and attach them across the frame, or from the edge of the frame and down to the background. See *Trees* by Pat Claybourne page 20. Backgrounds for embroidery are not always necessary, and here again a covered frame presents one with many possibilities.

9   Cover the ring of screw eyes with either whipping or buttonhole stitch, and screw them at irregular intervals round the inner edge of the frame. Through these suspend strong threads to form a base for needlewoven or buttonholed shapes. Additions of knitting, crochet, macramé, beads and cinemoid are very effective.

10   Instead of using screw eyes, sew threads through the fabric cover of the frame, remembering to take the thread round the edge of the frame occasionally for extra support. Lacy buttonhole is a very useful stitch for this method, and several layers of embroidery can be worked one above the other. See *Return To Earth* by Olga Catterson page 23.

'*Swamp*' *by Edith John*
Embroidery on a corner frame

16

'Cumbrian Clouds' by Winifred Shield
Fishing line supports for gauze clouds

'Foreshore' by Edith John
Lacy needleweaving worked from the top of a frame, over
padded appliqué and beadwork

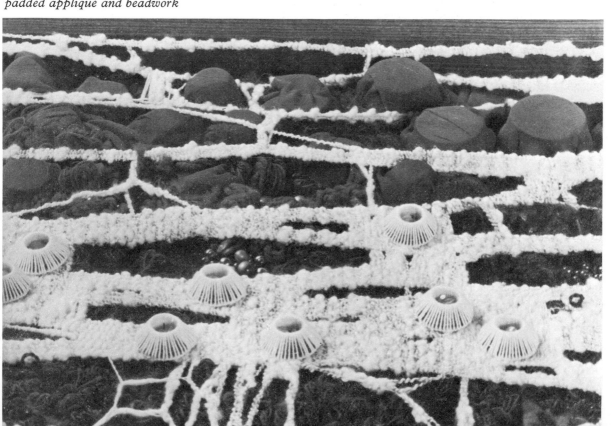

'Underwater Ballet' by Olga Catterson

'The Wave' by Edith John
Stitchery from the ground taken over the edge of the frame ▶

18

'Trees' by Pat Claybourne
Covered card shapes suspended across the frame

'Holes' by Joan Cook
Vilene support for upper layer of work

'Sunset' by Olga Catterson
Window embroidery

11 Embroidery worked without a background looks delightful with a light behind it, and if pieces of coloured acetate sheeting are inserted among the stitchery a stained glass effect is obtained. This method has given rise to a very practical use for framed embroidery, as it is possible to fix it to a window in place of short net curtaining. *Sunset* is a window embroidery, and besides illuminating the owner's staircase and giving her family pleasure, it is also a talking point for her neighbours.

It is now an easy step to combine several frames, say three, all the same size. Put a background into the first one and work it fairly heavily. Use the other two frames without a background and embroider them lightly so that it is possible to see clearly through each one. When the work is finished sew the frames one on top of the other, with the background frame at the bottom. Strengthen the sides by sticking and stitching a piece of fabric round them, and then put them into a glass fronted box. *Cumbrian Clouds* and *Holes* pages 17 and 21 are examples of this method.

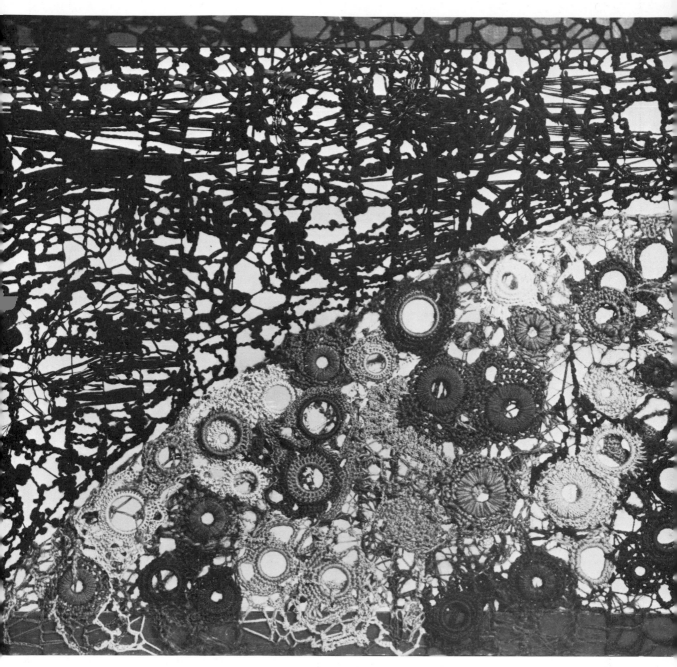

Detail from 'Return to Earth' by Olga Catterson
Embroidery without a background

2 Unusual supports for embroidery

We have discovered that a fabric background for embroidery is not absolutely essential, and in so doing we have widened the field for experimental work considerably. It can be enlarged still further if, instead of using a wooden frame to support our stitchery we look around and consider the possibilities of various man made objects. Those which are used for display purposes can be begged, borrowed or paid for once they are no longer required, or have been slightly damaged with rough usage. It is also profitable to examine the rubbish which is placed outside shops for the dustmen to collect. A great deal of apparently useless packing material consists of interesting shapes which make admirable foundations for embroidery. Friends and relatives, once they are aware of one's needs, will often save articles which would otherwise be thrown away. Make it a golden rule to accept every offering, no matter how useless it appears to be, because some day the despised object could easily become a treasure of great price.

Below are listed some of the treasures which have been used successfully by people of all ages, from fifteen year olds to really mature students.

1   Large glass bottles with stoppers, carboys and demijohns. These are generally embroidered on the outside with thick string, nylon cord or fine rope in a very open pattern of needleweaving, lacy buttonhole and other lace like stitches. Knitting, crochet and macramé can be incorporated in the design. See the diagrams. These glass objects make handsome lamp bases or containers for floral arrangements. Occasionally embroidered objects are suspended inside the bottle from the stopper. Plastic jars are useful too, but as they are so light they should be screwed to a heavy wooden base. See *String embroidered jar* by Jennifer Hutton.

2   Wire dartboard frames are good supports for embroidery and they have been used by young and mature students with equal success. This kind of background needs a more than usually interesting thread and the following ones have been found to be good. Strips of polythene, torn and frayed strips of cloth, weaving yarns, string, knitting yarns, rug yarns, and thick embroidery threads. Wooden beads, glass beads, sequins and covered washers, plus cinemoid are useful adjuncts. Fingers often prove to be better tools than needles, and the simplest stitches are

Page 25
String embroidered jar by
Jennifer Hutton
Note the embroidered fish bone.
This is to be suspended inside
the jar

the most effective. Try darning, whipping, herringbone, cretan, various chains and buttonhole. See dartboard frames by Margaret Stephens and Olive Smith.

3   Lampshade frames can be used for the construction of most unusual shades or for purely decorative pieces of work. It is rarely necessary to bind the frame, but on occasion binding does provide a firm ground for beginning and ending stitchery. See lampshade by Joan Cooper. This frame was bound, and then woollen threads were taken up and down the frame, and wrapped round the frame for about 13 mm ($\frac{1}{2}$ in.) between each length of thread, until an open background was complete. The background was decorated with freely worked needleweaving with a fairly heavy thread. Another layer of threads was arranged diagonally over this weaving and used as a background for a much lacier pattern of Finnish needleweaving.

A gathered silk lining was added, and the top and bottom of the lampshade were neatened with a knitted braid.

Traditional Finnish needle-weaving
(a) After the second row proceed as for row 2, and interlace each row with its predecessor
(b) Whip openly the first group only from ● to the top. Then whip and interlace from the top downwards

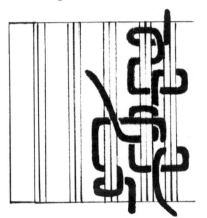

● BEGIN HERE

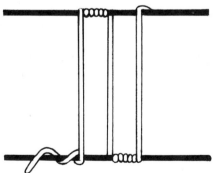

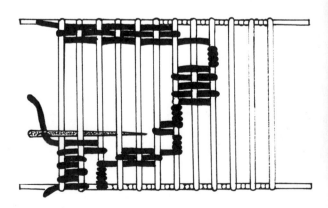

Weaving on a lampshade frame
(a) Wrap a strong thread over the lampshade frame
(b) Darn alternately over and under the threads and make a lacy pattern

Dartboard frame by Olive Smith

Dartboard frame by Margaret Stephens

Lampshade by Joan Cooper

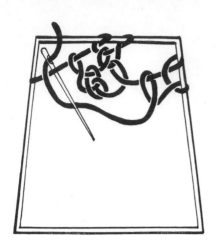

Lacy buttonhole on a lampshade frame. Buttonhole firmly but not too lightly, and make a lacy pattern

Lampshade by Pat Byrne is most unusual. She chose to embroider the frame with lacy buttonhole using fine copper wire as her thread. The frame needed no binding as the wire could be twisted firmly round the struts. A central cylinder made of a copper tile with holes cut in it was placed in position before the outer embroidery was worked. With a small coloured bulb, and a rough piece of slate for a base, this shade is both decorative and useful. It would make an excellent night light for a child, or an invalid, or serve in more romantic circumstances on a dinner table.

Lampshade by Pat Byrne

Facing page

Lampshade by Olive Smith

Lampshade by Olive Smith is purely decorative. It was embroidered with glossy raffia and curtain rings covered with buttonhole stitch. Between the outer wall and an inner cylinder discs of *melinex* (acetate) were suspended on nylon thread.

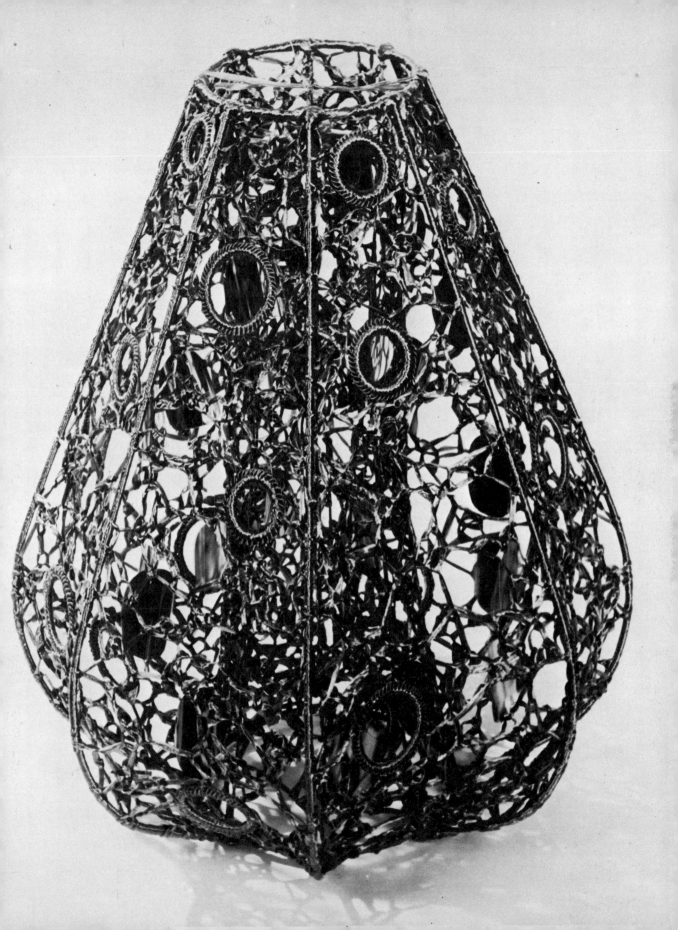

Vegetable bag lampshade by Mary Paulucy

Seedhead by Edith John is another purely decorative unit worked on a lampshade frame. It can be suspended in space or used as a free standing embroidery. The stitchery, lacy buttonhole, was worked with weaving yarns, and the knobs were made of covered rings and extra large metal eyelets.

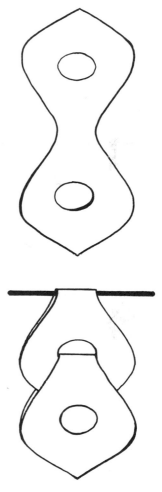

'Seedhead' by Edith John

The centre piece was built up on the plastic core from a ball of knitting cotton. Other ideas for practical and unusual lampshades were evolved by Wendy Greenfield, Janet Craggs, Noreen Swindell and Florence Semper.

Wendy Greenfield bound a frame and covered it with chiffon. Then she made numerous small bags of two pieces of fabric padded with 6 mm ($\frac{1}{4}$ in.) foam, in tones of orange and red. Some were embroidered and some were beaded. These bags were stitched at random on the chiffon, and beads of an exactly matching colour concealed the stitches inside the shade. Some of the bags were placed so that they extended beyond the edges of the frame, and narrow channels were left between all the bags to allow the light to show through the cover.

Noreen Swindell first bound a frame, and covered the uprights with macramé. Then, using the shape as shown in the diagram, she cut from iron-on *vilene* numerous pieces of different sizes. She ironed these pieces to her fabric, leaving plenty of space between them. Most of the pieces were cut with no turnings, but on a few she left 13 mm ($\frac{1}{2}$ in.) of fabric beyond the *vilene* and frayed it out. Then some of the pieces were lightly embroidered on the sewing machine, after which all the pieces were linked to form a shade, beginning at the top edge of the frame which was placed inside the fold of the first row. A delicate lining was added and hand made beads completed the shade.

(a) Use the pattern and cut as many pieces as needed, in different sizes
(b) Fold the first piece over the top edge of the lampshade frame, then link the pieces as shown

Janet Craggs made a disposable shade for children, teenagers and those who like frequent changes in their environment. She made it of layers of newspaper glued together with *polycell*. A second frame she covered with delicate lacy buttonhole, then down the uprights she fixed a stiffened wavy piece of machine embroidered fabric. The shade looked most interesting when light shone through it.

Lampshade by Janet Craggs

Vilene Bondaweb, sold in packs 914 mm × 203 mm (36 in. × 8 in.) is another fabric which releases lampshade makers from many difficulties. It can be fused between two layers of fabric, making it possible to use paper sculpture techniques, as the fabric is rendered firm, pliable and almost fray proof. Jennifer Morgan produced a charming lampshade by this method.

Pin art, which has been so popular and which is supplied in kits, inspired Florence Semper to make a delicate lampshade. She bound a frame, then stitched round it beads of various sizes about 13 mm ($\frac{1}{2}$ in.) apart all round the frame. She then made her lacy pattern with lurex flecked thread, using the beads instead of panel pins. When the work was complete she sealed the threads where they passed round the beads with *marvin medium*. A lining was added to conceal the bulb.

4   Huge cardboard rings, either 76 mm or 152 mm (3 in. or 6 in.) deep, which are used for display purposes, present a challenge to the ingenuity of the embroiderer. *Ring* (facing page 24) is a most successful effort. The ring was covered inside and out with a plain fabric, and then a second cover was worked with coarse crochet in several colours. This crochet was stretched tightly round the

'Diamond Wedding' by Edith John

outside and inside and joined with stitchery round the rim of the hoop. From this crochet strong threads were arranged firmly across the interior and freely worked with needleweaving. Additional decoration made by covering large plastic washers with buttonhole, and delicate tufts of frayed string completed the work.

Diamond Wedding was worked on a 152 mm (6 in.) deep ring. The outside was covered with tightly stretched furnishing fabric, and the inside was given a softer look by lining it with gathered crystal nylon. From front to back inside the ring Finnish needleweaving of glossy raffia was criss-crossed so that a diamond shaped space was left empty in the centre. A long diamond made of fabric covered triangles of card was held firmly across this space with nylon thread which was taken right through the hoop and fixed securely on the outside. The outside was decor-

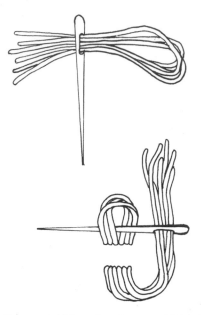

Cut several lengths of yarn, fold
them in half and take the loose
ends through the eye of the
needle. Pass the needle through
the ground and into the loop.
Pull the ends tightly to make a
knot. Repeat as often as necessary

Barrel tops by Amanda Francis

ated with needleweaving to match the centre. The back
was closed with a piece of felt covered card, on the inside
of which a large square of mirror was stuck.

5   Polystyrene shapes are easily obtainable, and make good
supporters for embroidery. Since they are very light they
are ideal for mobiles, but they can be fixed to a heavy
foundation if free standing work is required. These shapes
can be covered with a stretchy fabric such as crimplene or
felt, and the embroidery may be added either before or
after the cloth is sewn round them.

6   The tops of wooden barrels with a hole in the centre
can be painted, polished or stained before use. Choose a
thick soft string and tie it through the hole and proceed
with finger embroidery to decorate the shape. Two or
three different sizes may be linked together, as shown in
the photograph *Barrel Tops* by Amanda Francis. These
were joined by overlapping them over cotton reels, to
which they were nailed.

7   Wire spark guards which have been relegated to the
attic after the installation of central heating offer great
scope. The mesh should be treated like canvas or openly
woven linen. Tufting, darning, padded appliqué and almost any kind of stitchery are suitable. See *Shaggy Look*
by Alan Abbey and the diagram on page 92 for tufting, for
ideas for this background.

8   Plastic lettuce shakers and colanders make interesting
bases. A successful quilted, beaded and stitched mask was
built up on a lettuce shaker and of course hanging was no
problem. A background is not always required as the holes
in these objects can be stitched through.

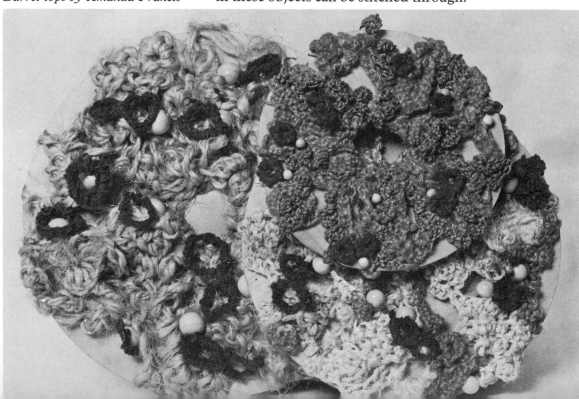

9 Old bicycle wheels, cleaned and stripped of their tyres, make firm backgrounds for embroidery with cinemoid, strips of polythene, strips of fabric, feathers, string, foil, baubles and raffia. Macramé, knitting and crochet are also useful for filling gaps or making a base on which to work. Suspended by the hub from a ceiling and under the lights, decorated wheels create a charming effect in large areas such as school halls.

10 Furniture is another source of support for creative embroidery. Fold away and stacking chairs with canvas or plastic seats and backs often need repairing, and so do old wooden chairs with hollow backs and seats. Use thick soft string, nylon cord or rope to create a strong but lace-like filling in the parts which have lost their original covers. Embroidery of this kind may be added between the legs of dining chairs, or to cane furniture which has seen better days. This work is quick, durable, effective and easily replaced.

11 Surely there must be many strong and elegant hat boxes gathering dust in attics. The cardboard variety can be utilised for free standing embroidery in many ways. Cut large holes in the sides of the box, then cover it with fabric as suggested in Chapter 1 and shown in the diagram on page 14. Cut a piece of fabric for the base with a 13 mm ($\frac{1}{2}$ in.) turning. Snip and press the turning, then pin the fabric in place and sew it to the fabric on the side of the box. If the base should be hollow first fill it with a pad of foam, to make a flat, firm surface, and then cover it. The lid need not be lined. Simply pad it up with foam in any way desired on the top and sides. Cover it with a gathered circle of cloth to which rich embroidery has been added. Turn the edge in during the gathering process and then there will be no need to glue the edge of the fabric to the inside of the lid. Attach it with invisible stitches through the card. Now make gay mobiles using lots of sequins and suspend them on fishing line from the inside of the lid. Press the lid into position, and as it will be a very tight fit great care should be taken not to break its side. A smear of *copydex* on the inside of the rim of the lid will secure it. Many alternatives to the foregoing idea are possible, and it remains for those who are interested to develop this simple theme.

12 Hair brushes and hand mirrors for dressing tables often have plain smooth backs. Work some embroidery on a fabric which can be mounted on a piece of thin card. Stick this to the back of the toilet articles with *copydex* and when it is dry coat the whole surface with *marvin medium* and leave it to dry out. Do not get this wet when cleaning the brush.

3 Manipulating fabrics

Fabrics are many and various, and as some are made specifically for certain kinds of embroidery, we tend to accept them at their face value. Rarely is it considered to be an essential part of experimental embroidery to discover first the hidden talents in a piece of cloth.

1   Consider man made fabrics. A touch with a hot iron and they either melt, or harden into a toffee like consistency, or scorch and turn yellowish brown. This is probably a disaster to someone who is making a dress, but to the embroiderer it should be a revelation. Deliberate scorching can do wonders for a plain coloured fabric, especially if it is so constituted that some of the threads refuse to scorch. To melt or harden chosen areas, especially if splitting occurs, provides unusual pieces for appliqué.

2   If such drastic treatment of fabric seems to be going too far, consider something gentler. Most loosely woven fabrics can be textured either regularly or at random by moving the threads with the fingers, or by first pushing a stiletto, a pencil or a knitting needle between them and then pulling them apart. See illustrations on page 40. This method can be used as an end in itself, but plain machined lines or simple hand stitchery helps to keep the threads in place. Practical uses for this method are numerous such as dress decoration, lampshades, curtains, cushions and panels.

3   Another way to texture a fabric is to ease, but not withdraw threads, at irregular intervals, in one or both directions. This creates a bubbly effect and it looks particularly good on chiffon, georgette and all soft transparent fabrics. It does work successfully on many heavier fabrics too. One can see that this would make lovely decoration for dresses, especially those which are meant for romantic occasions. Look at the clouds in *Sky* by Charlotte Wellborne page 41. They were cut much larger than required from a piece of chiffon, and the edges were frayed. Then threads were eased across the fabric in both directions until it was small enough to fit the pattern which was drawn on the background fabric. The edges were pinned in place and then fixed with running stitch with fine gold thread. Invisible stitches placed at random among the bubbles controlled them sufficiently. It may be said in passing that Charlotte Wellborne is nearly eighty years old and that before she embarked on her embroidery she first painted a sky which she saw from her dining room window.

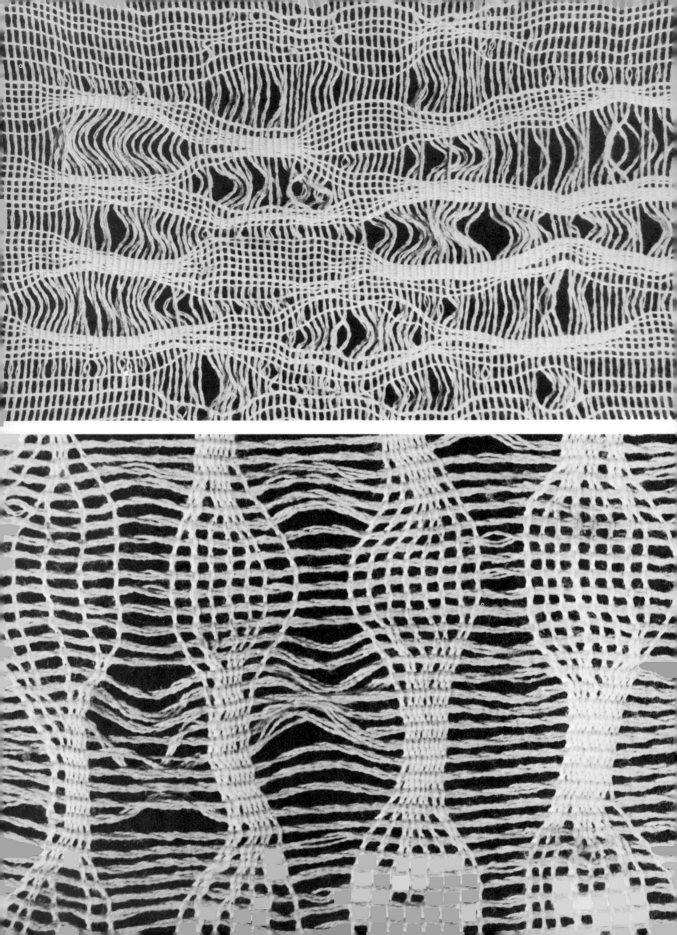

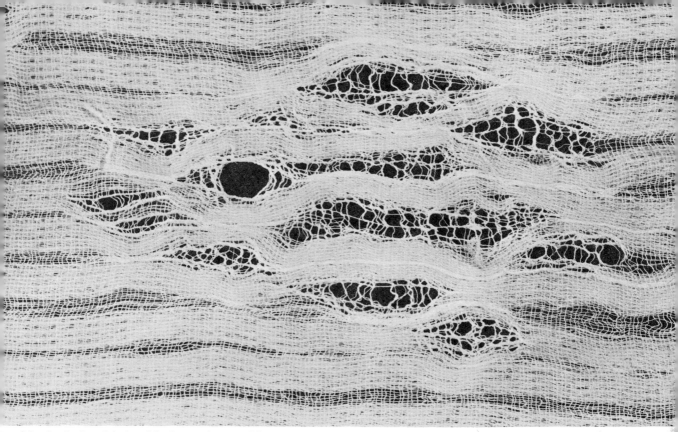

Manipulating fabric with the sewing machine by Mary Paulucy

◄ *Manipulating Scandinavian fabric*
Manipulating Scandinavian fabric

'Sky' by Mary Wellborne

This method is quite practical, as a glance at Sheila Barker's pulpit fall will prove. Here the flames were made in the same way as the clouds mentioned above, then overlaid on the cross and held in position with a number of invisible stitches.

4 The next venture is to cut holes in fabric. This idea seems to shock many people in spite of the continuing appeal of many traditional forms of cut work. If one considers the following suggestions to be ideas for the development of cut work it is easier to take the scissors and snip away light-heartedly.

(a) Frame a piece of medium weight fabric and mark on it several similar shapes of dissimilar sizes. Cut out the holes leaving 15 mm (about ½ in.) turning inside each shape. Snip the turning then lightly stick or sew it to the wrong side of the work. See diagram on page 14 and photograph to left. Put down some firm foundation threads and take them through the holes, linking them together. Weave with textured and smooth yarns.

(b) Loosely woven fabrics which have a knitted or twisted weave do not usually fray easily and they can be slit quite safely. The piece of furnishing fabric shown in photograph on this page is ideal for modern cut work. Slits of irregular length were cut at random across the twisted threads, and then the background was decorated with rows and rows of finely worked herringbone stitch pulled tight. On reaching a slit its edge was rolled forward and incorporated in the embroidery. This piece of work is firm and strong and is quite practical. For perfect control and good technique a frame is necessary.

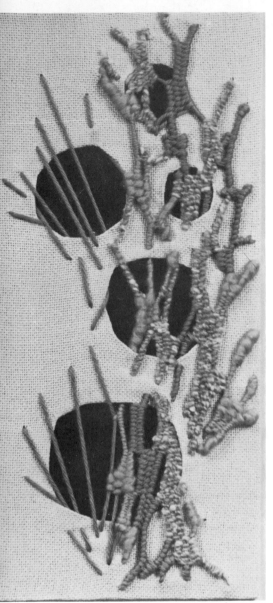

Needleweaving with holes
New look cut work on white fabric

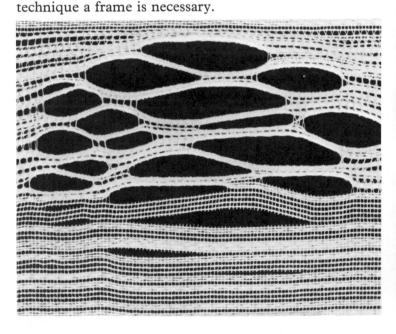

Facing page
Pulpit fall by Sheila Barker
Ruched chiffon

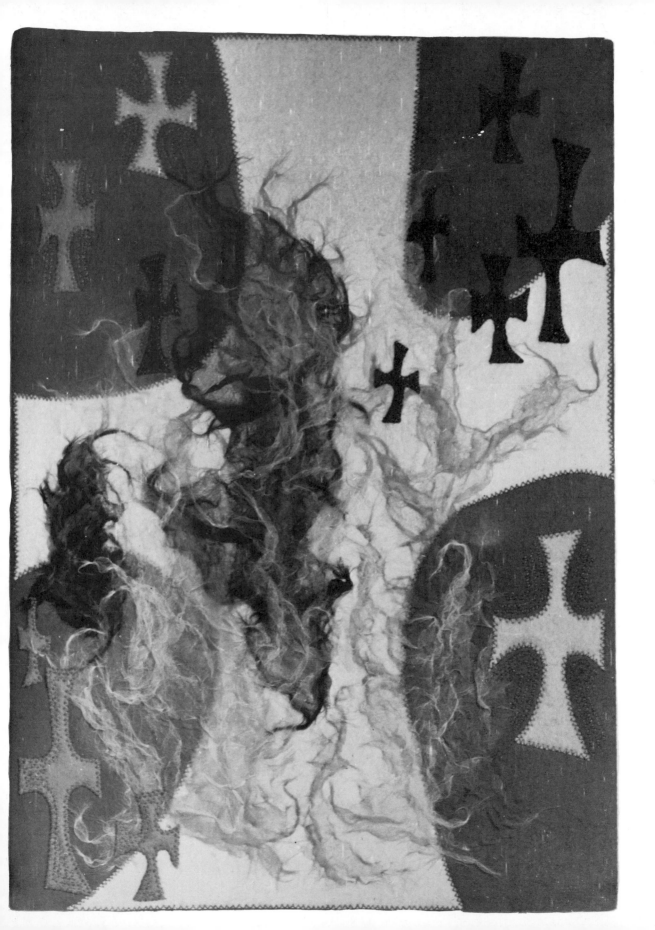

(c)   Cheese cloth makes an interesting background. Holes cut in it can be made quite secure by rolling the edge forward and sewing it invisibly. Because this fabric is so elastic it is ideal for freely worked pulled stitches, and by gathering circles of various sizes the surface can be made quite knobbly. The knobs can be heightened by pushing wadding into them from the back before the gathering stitches are tightened. Threads may be cut to allow the fabric to run, which gives a lacy effect, and torn or frayed strips of chiffon or other gauze like fabrics can be darned into the runs. The ends of the strips may be left hanging in soft bunches.

Experiment on cheese cloth

5   To go even further than mere burning or slashing, take a piece of loosely woven fabric, such as two toned curtaining, and literally pull it to pieces by withdrawing all the threads in one direction except for a small area at one end. Gather, pleat, or otherwise crumple the whole area and sew it with the threads which were withdrawn. Take the loose ends and plait, cord, or use macramé techniques. This will now make a pleasant wall hanging if it is suitably mounted. See *Hanging* by Judith Johnstone. Other ideas for the use of this kind of work will present themselves, and as silly as it seems beautiful sashes, scarves, bell pulls and lampshades can be made by this method.

Hanging by Judith Johnstone

45

Manipulating fabric does not necessarily mean destroying it in order to create something new.

6   A little girl pulled a small vegetable bag over her head as she was playing, and her mother instantly saw that it could be embroidered into a very stylish hat. She took thick and fluffy weaving yarns and darned and wove, pulling the threads of the bag apart as she did so. The result can be seen in the photograph of the *Hat* by Pat Byrne.

If threads of some vegetable bags are snipped and then pulled, a long slit appears and its ends can be closed by knotting the cut ends. The result is decorative and suggests that it can be used for lampshades and other items. Vegetable bags can be needlewoven without withdrawing threads and of course they are suitable for pulled work too. Since they are cheap, pretty and strong, in these days of rising prices they should not be ignored.

7   Another parent took a length of loosely woven *dralon*, folded it in half, and with virtually no cutting she constructed a smart garment for her daughter by tucking, smocking and pulling threads. See photograph of *Smart Girl* by Janet Craggs page 48.

There is another method of exploring materials which is not very difficult, but it does require patience, and it entails in the initial stages a certain amount of waste. It is concerned with woven fabrics, and in order to begin it is necessary to collect quite an assortment from fine to coarse, from silk to wool and man made pieces. The idea is to withdraw threads from either warp or weft, or both, and hope for something interesting to happen.

8   A piece of twill woven cloth suddenly became fascinating after two threads had been withdrawn and one left, alternately down 100 mm (4 in.) of a strip. It was found that there remained three layers of fabric, one and three composed of upright threads and the middle one of open tabby weaving. See photograph page 48.

It was decided to cut away the top layer by cutting the threads down the centre and darning the ends back. At this stage the cloth was ready to be embroidered. Suggestions for the embroidery included hem stitching, pulled work, needleweaving and hardanger fillings.

9   From satin woven fabrics it is possible to cut away whole areas of the top threads and find a complete fabric of another colour and/or texture beneath.

Perhaps some of the most interesting results have come from experiments with simple, evenly woven fabrics like Glenshee Egyptian Cotton and coarse evenweave cloth. Coarse fabrics are suggested for those who have never tried the following ideas, but of course experienced needlewomen will choose the kind of fabric they prefer.

Facing page
Hat by Pat Byrne

Page 48
'Smart girl' by Janet Craggs

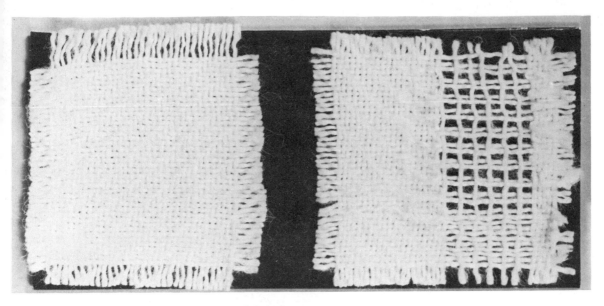

Above. Three layers from a twill weave fabric

Below left. Three layers
Below right. Chequerboard needleweaving

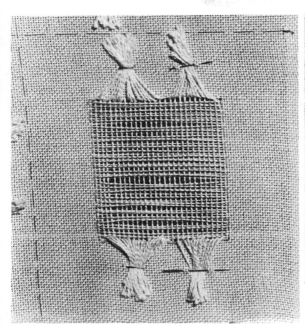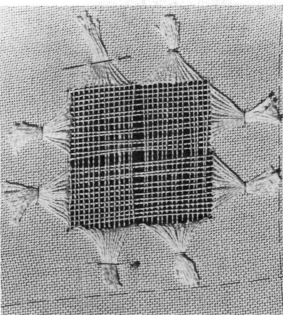

10   Frame up a 406 mm (16 in.) square of coarse, evenly woven fabric, and divide it into four with lines tacked down the middle from top to bottom and side to side. In each quarter, true to the thread, tack a 76 mm (3 in.) square.

(a)   In square one snip every other thread up the centre from bottom to top. Draw the cut threads carefully to the sides of the square and pin, tack or fix them with *sellotape* as a temporary measure. See photograph. There are now three layers of fabric, two upright layers with a horizontal one between them.

(b)   In square two repeat this process, then snip the top threads across the centre and fasten them back. There are now two layers, one horizontal and one vertical.

(c)   Find the centre of square three and cut two threads together. This is called a deliberate mistake. On each side of the mistake leave a thread and cut a thread alternately to the edges of the square. Draw the cut threads to the sides and fix them back. It will be found that where the mistake was made the three layers of fabric interlock. Slip a pencil under the top layer and cut all the threads as near to the centre as possible. Half of the cut threads will stay on top, and half of them will drop underneath the work. Draw the under threads to the surface at the edge of the square and fasten all the loose ends as before.

(d)   Square four is begun exactly like square three, but after cutting the first layer of threads and fixing them over the sides, pause and collect two pencils. Beginning at the right side of the top layer insert a pencil under half of the threads. From the left side take the remaining half of the threads on the second pencil. See photograph. Cut the threads on each pencil as near to the centre as possible. Again, some will stay on top of the work and some will drop beneath it. Draw the under threads to the top and fasten down all the loose ends. Now you will have what is known as a chequer board, and it was devised by Nellie Bergh of New York. She reasoned that if a deliberate mistake when cutting the first layer of threads produces interlacing of the fabric, a deliberate mistake in both directions would produce squares.

See photograph for the results when embroidery is added.

It now remains to add the embroidery, which usually takes the form of needleweaving, whipping, or hemstitching. It is difficult to embroider square one, and it has been found best to work on the top layer first, with very simple and very open embroidery. The second layer can now be seen clearly and should be embroidered simply and openly. Layer three is done from the back of the work, and

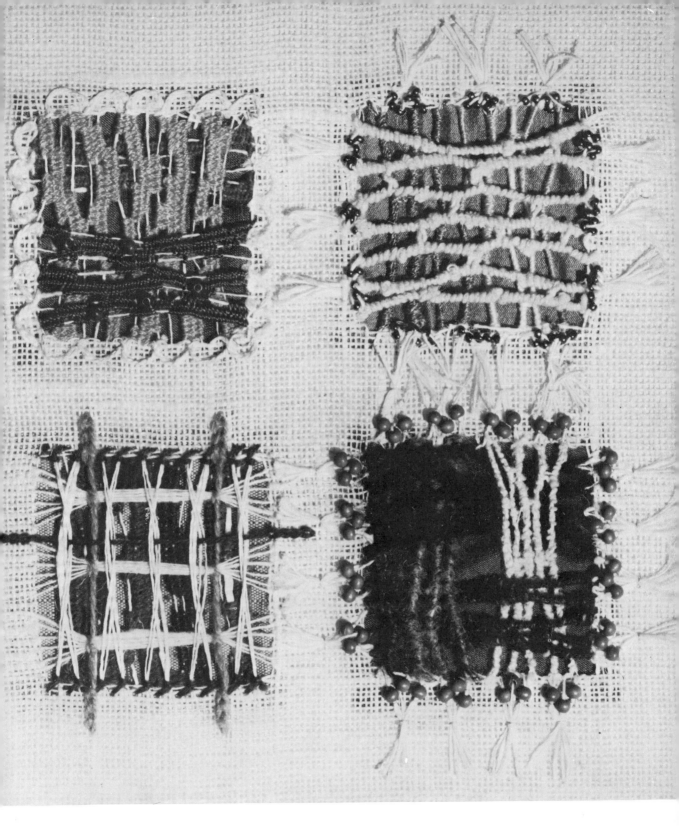

Completed squares by Mary Paulucy

is usually but not necessarily made heavier and closer than the other two.

From this point the embroiderer should experiment for herself, but here follow a few suggestions for further development. Fabric in which the warp and weft are of different colours is pleasant when used for squares three and four, especially when all the foundation threads are not completely covered with embroidery. Long, narrow panels with three or four deliberate mistakes in one or both directions give really splendid results. These methods can be worked in circles or any other shape. See photograph of *Circle* by Mary Paulucy. The next five photographs show a few more variations.

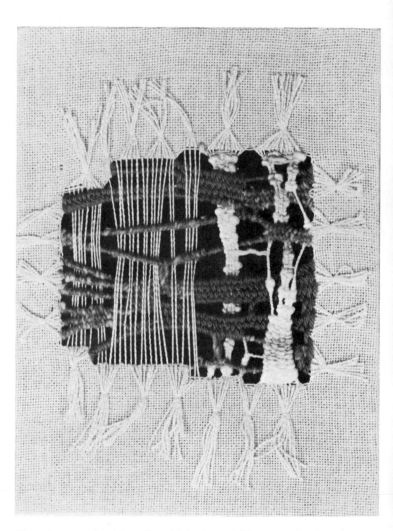

Two-layer embroidery in which three deliberate mistakes were made

'Circle' by Mary Paulucy
Chequer board

A variation of three-layer embroidery. Weave layers one and three together and leave the middle layer exposed

A three-layer border. The second layer was halved and pushed aside by using single twist clustering to hold one and three together

Three layers of threads were laid with different coloured cottons and then woven

Two layers of threads were placed at irregular intervals on the fabric, and both were woven at random

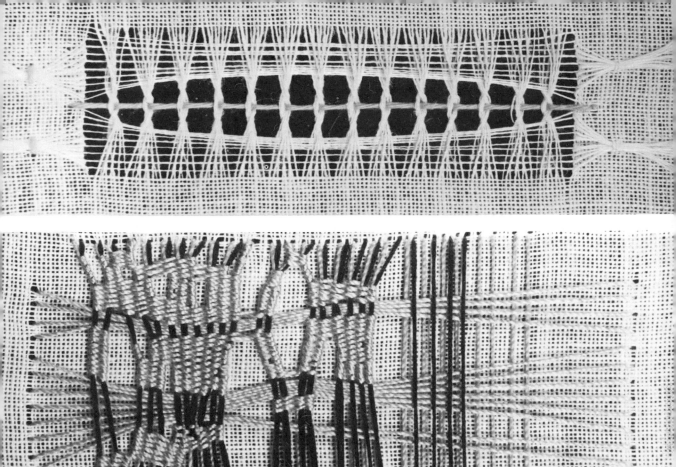

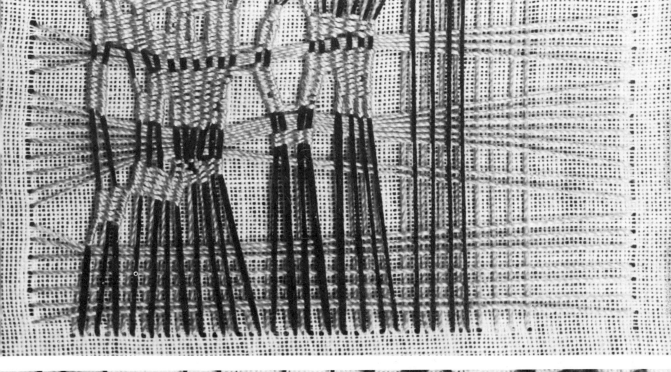

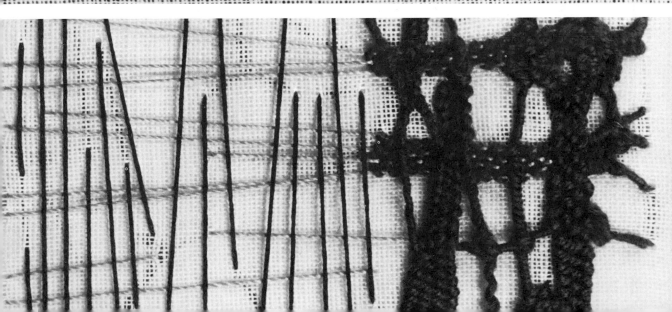

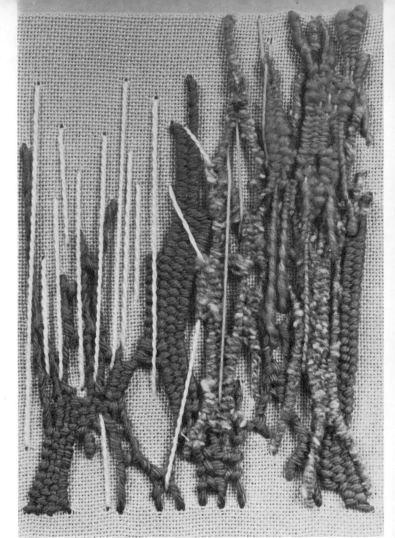

Three-layer weaving

For those who prefer to cut threads in a free fashion the following idea has much to offer, as it allows a lovely curvaceous rendering of a design which is similar to Art Nouveau. Natural form can be suggested with this kind of weaving without the stiff, squared effect which results from most needleweaving.

Free cutting of threads

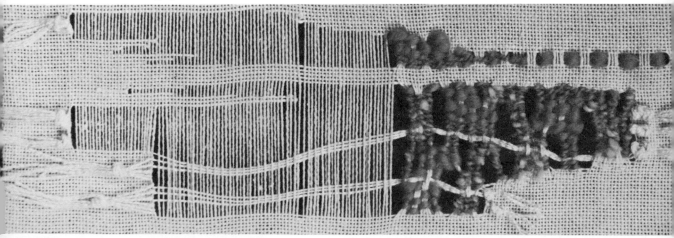

11 Decide on the shape which is to be embroidered and tack the outlines as a guide. Beginning in the middle of the shape cut threads at random, several at a time, and occasionally every other one. When alternate threads are cut the remainder slide easily into any position. Study the photograph on page 56 which shows clearly how loose ends are left, and then packed so tightly among the needle-weaving that there is no fear of them working loose.

All that remains to be said now is how to dispose of those ends which were fastened back during the weaving process. The traditional way is to darn them back into the material for about 25 mm and cut off the ends. A glance at the photographs will show that there are many other methods, and no doubt readers will think of better ones.

Cutting, tearing, burning and rumpling materials may not have a universal appeal, in spite of their undoubted value in experimental work, so we will turn now to a less violent but none the less exciting method of manipulation.

Soft gloving leathers and suédes, soft and easily stitched metallic leather, soft imitation leather, felt and some bonded fabrics are all used in appliqué for ecclesiastical and domestic embroideries. They are usually applied flat or slightly padded, but their charm is greatly enhanced if they are modelled by simple cutting and stitching.

12 Old fashioned punching has something to offer modern needlewomen too, as will be gathered from the following suggestions.

(a) Punch a piece of leather at random, and keep the punched pieces. Apply the leather to the ground and then scatter the dots over and around it.

(b) Punch a piece of leather and partly sew it into position. Then, using a very large chenille needle thread Japanese gold or imitation gold, through the holes and under the leather. Finish sewing the applied piece.

(c) Punch the leather and apply it, then replace the dots over but slightly to one side of the holes.

(d) Apply, without punching, a piece of leather. Then punch dozens of dots from a spare piece of the same leather, and stitch them over the appliqué to texture it.

(e) The leather from which dots have been punched resembles sequin waste. Never throw it away. Use it for its own sake, or cut it into pleasant shapes and apply them over plain pieces of leather or any other fabric.

(f) Punched leather looks interesting when beads and sequins are sewn into the holes.

(g) Punch all over a fairly large piece of leather and save the dots. Cut several similar shapes from the punched piece and apply them so that they overlap. This gives a slightly padded look to the work, and the holes take on

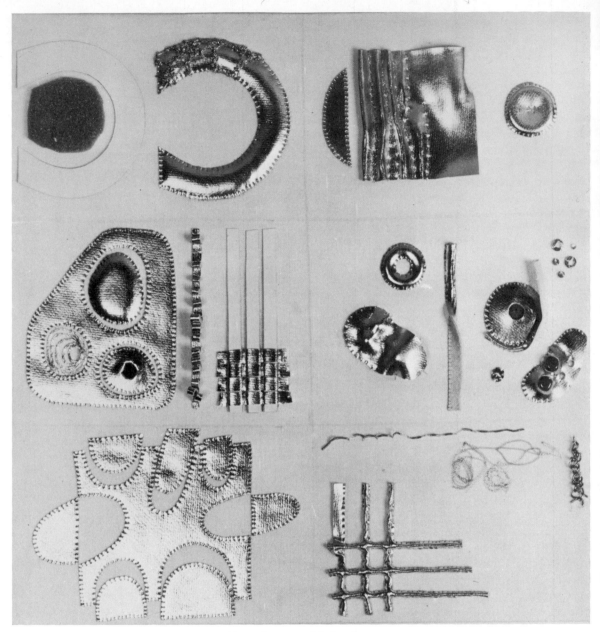

Experiments with leather

different shapes as one piece of leather partly blocks another. Sprinkle the dots around to soften the outline. See the photographs.

13   Beads can be sewn on the ground under soft leather appliqué. Cut the leather slightly larger than required, stretch it over the beads and sew it down. Then add little stitches at random among the beads to stretch the leather still further. This method gives an interesting knobbly surface to the leather.

14 Semi-precious stones may be stuck to the background, then the piece of leather which is to be applied is placed over the stones so that their position can be marked on it with a needle. Cut a hole smaller than each stone, and then sew the leather in place over them. Stretch the leather slightly over each stone, and where necessary add a few tiny stitches to hold it firmly in place. This gives the effect of jewelled pewter work on boxes which was so popular during the 30s. See photograph.

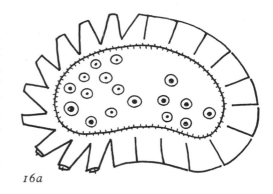

16a

15 Scraps of leather which are left after cutting out larger pieces can be used to build up good designs. They rarely need re-cutting, as careful placing is all that is required. Therefore nothing of these expensive materials need be wasted.

16 Now turn to *Light* and *Dark* on page 61. One simple shape, in different sizes, was cut out five times, and for the sake of experiment each was treated in a different manner.

(a) Beginning at the top left. Cut out a piece of leather as shown in diagram 16, and from it cut out a centre piece leaving an edge 19 mm ($\frac{3}{4}$ in.) wide. Sew down the small piece and decorate it with leather dots and beads. Take the remaining piece and cut slits in it 13 mm ($\frac{1}{2}$ in.) long, and leave 13 mm ($\frac{1}{2}$ in.) between them. Place this piece round the central area and stitch it on the inner edge. Take each flap in turn and fold one edge under, making a triangular point. Fasten the under piece with one stitch near the point only as this is sufficient to hold the edge firm.

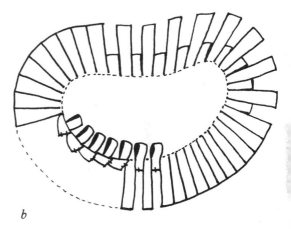

b

(b) Top right. Fringe the edge of this piece of leather by making slits in it 25 mm (1 in.) long and 6 mm ($\frac{1}{4}$ in.) apart. Sew the leather to the background and put one stitch in each slit. Push alternate ends of the fringe right up to the main piece and catch with one stitch. Pull the remaining pieces round those already stitched and hold them in position with two stitches.

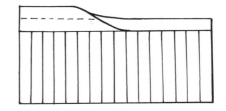

(c) Centre. Punch the leather at random and replace some of the dots, holding them in position either with a stitch or a bead. Take a straight piece of very soft leather 50 mm (2 in.) wide and long enough to go round the shape. Fringe this piece to within 13 mm ($\frac{1}{2}$ in.) of the top, then paste the top edge on the wrong side and fold it over, making a 6 mm ($\frac{1}{4}$ in.) deep collar. Place this fringe round the main piece so that the collar makes a raised edge, and catch the inner edge of the collar to the background. Neatly join the ends. The ends of the fringe may be held in place with a bead.

(d) Bottom left. Take a piece of very soft gloving leather and cut it 25 mm (1 in.) larger all round than the pattern. Cut out a small circular hole as indicated and save the spare piece of leather. Stick rubber or plastic rings to the background, avoiding the area of the hole. Place the leather in

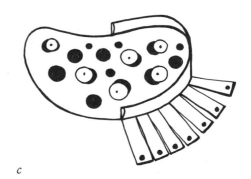

c

59

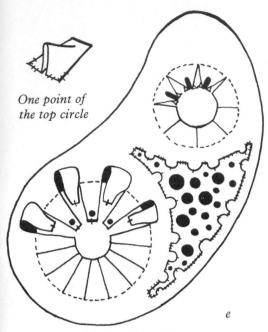

*One point of
the top circle*

Light and Dark

Explode paper circle

*Fill each portion with
different leathers*

position and fix with five or six stitches spaced round the edge. Gently pull, ease, and push the leather into folds over and into the rings and fix the folds with lots of little invisible stitches. Stick a pad of 6 mm ($\frac{1}{4}$ in.) foam in the hole and stitch over it the spare piece of leather.

(e)   Bottom right. Cut two small circles from this piece of leather and keep them on one side. Snip the edge of the top hole eight times to a depth of 13 mm ($\frac{1}{2}$ in.) and snip the bottom one sixteen times to a depth of 25 mm (1 in.). Sew this prepared leather to the background. The points of the eight flaps should be squeezed together and stitched, then replace the piece of leather in the hole, and add beads. Push alternate flaps of the lower hole right up to the edge and stitch in place. Leave the remaining flaps flat and stitch them and add a bead at the end. Replace the spare piece in the hole and stitch down. Cut a curved triangle of punched leather and sew it between the holes, decorating it with round and shiny beads.

(f)   For the rest of the sampler use waste pieces of leather and soft thongs.

17   More ways of padding and manipulating leather can be seen in *Laudate* by Edith John, and *Sunflower* by Dorothy Petty overleaf. The top of the wings in *Laudate* and the leaves round the edge of *Sunflower* were lined with leather, and soft wire was stuck between the two pieces, along the upper edge. It was possible to mould the wings and leaves into the desired position, and very few stitches were needed to make them secure.

Three methods were used for the angels' skirts, which were made with very soft gloving leather.

(a)   The leather was cut much wider than the pattern and gathered on the upper edge until it was the right size. Then the leather was stitched round the edges, after which it was pulled into folds, which were then sewn in place.

(b)   Rubber rings were used as padding and the skirt was made larger than the pattern in order to accommodate them.

(c)   Squares of 6 mm ($\frac{1}{4}$ in.) foam were stuck at random under the leather, which was eased and stitched over them. Each pad was then decorated with a large jewel.

18   There are countless ways of developing simple circular shapes of leather into most interesting units.

(a)   Cut a fairly large circle from a piece of paper and explode it into pieces. Mark the original circle on a piece of fabric, and cut the exploded shapes from a piece of leather. Now sew them in position; pad some, ruche some, leave some flat. Try using more than one kind of leather, as the contrast in texture and colouring is pleasing.

(b)   Cut a ring of leather 19 mm ($\frac{3}{4}$ in.) deep and 100 mm

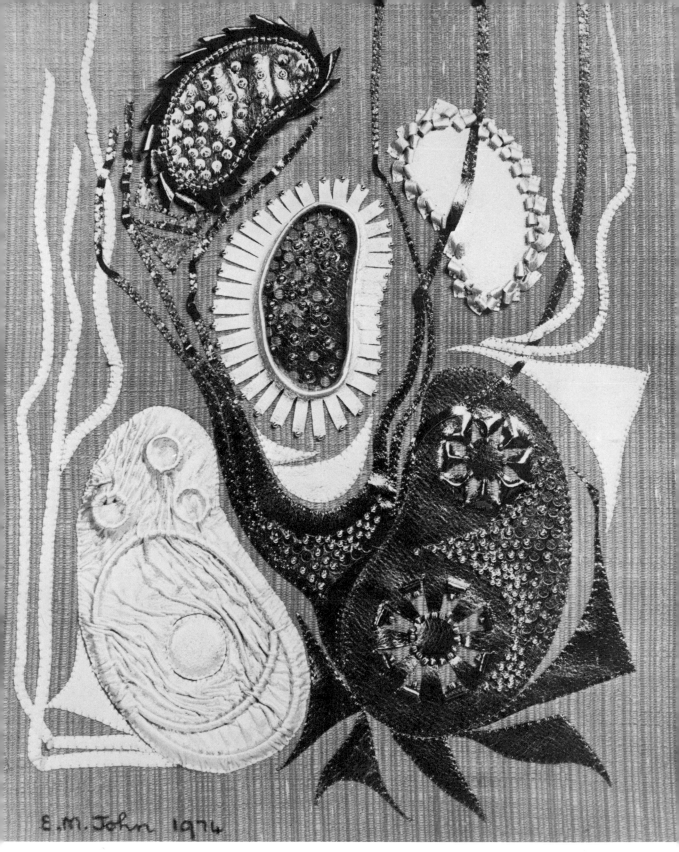

E. M. John 1974

'Light and Dark' by Edith John

'*Laudate*' *by Edith John*

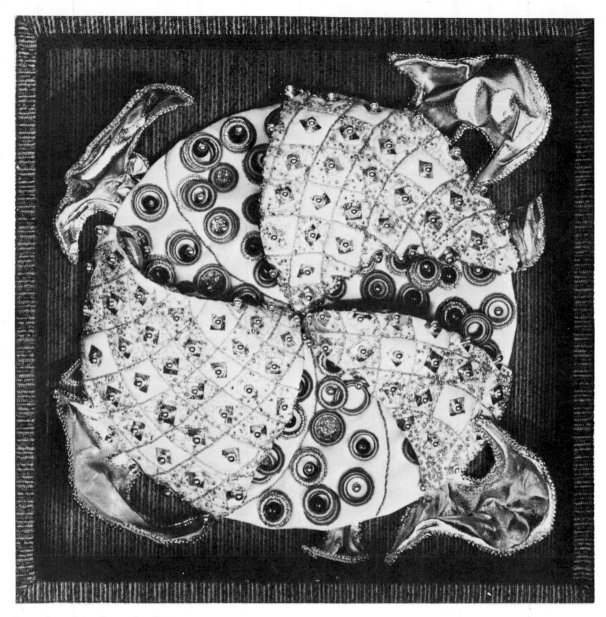

'Sunflower' by Dorothy Petty

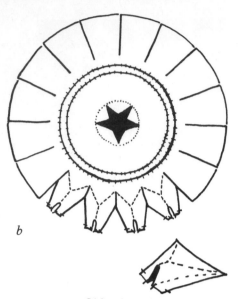

b

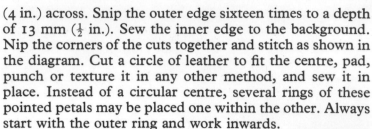

(4 in.) across. Snip the outer edge sixteen times to a depth of 13 mm ($\frac{1}{2}$ in.). Sew the inner edge to the background. Nip the corners of the cuts together and stitch as shown in the diagram. Cut a circle of leather to fit the centre, pad, punch or texture it in any other method, and sew it in place. Instead of a circular centre, several rings of these pointed petals may be placed one within the other. Always start with the outer ring and work inwards.

(c)   Cut a circle of leather 152 mm (6 in.) in diameter, and from the centre of it cut out a circle 38 mm (1$\frac{1}{2}$ in.) in diameter. Slit the outer edge of the large piece sixteen times to a depth of 57 mm (2$\frac{1}{4}$ in.). Stitch the inner edge to the background. Nip the ends of the fringed pieces and stitch as shown in the diagram.

Now cut a circle 89 mm (3$\frac{1}{2}$ in.) in diameter, take out a centre 19 mm ($\frac{3}{4}$ in.) in diameter. Slit the edges sixteen times to a depth of 32 mm (1$\frac{1}{4}$ in.). Place it inside the first ring so that the cut pieces fall between the outer petals, and sew as described above. Sew beads at the ends of the petals and decorate the centre with beads or stitches.

(d)   Cut six circles with a diameter of 25 mm (1 in.) and fold them from the wrong side as shown in the diagram. Place them on the background to form a circular flower, with the folded edges meeting in the centre of it. Stick the folded edges of one petal to those of its neighbour, and stitch the outer edges in place.

(e)   Cut a large circle, and then cut a ring 25 mm (1 in.) deep from its edge. Snip the outer edge of the ring sixteen times and place on one side. Cut several holes in the remaining circle, leaving about 25 mm (1 in.) at least between these holes, and 25 mm (1 in.) from the edge. Sew this circle to the background and stitch round the holes. Edge each hole with a ring of eight pointed petals as described at (b), and then replace the outer ring, which should be treated in the same way.

Side view of points
For small shapes only four
stitches are needed

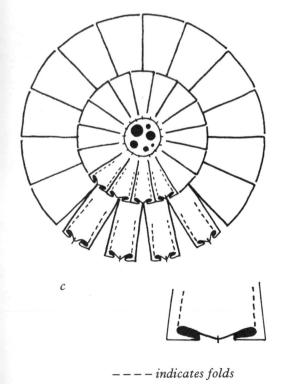

c

— — — — indicates folds

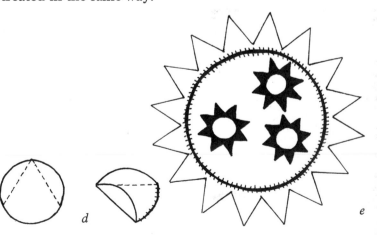

d

e

19   Strips of leather from 3 mm ($\frac{1}{8}$ in.) wide to 13 mm ($\frac{1}{2}$ in.) or any other required size have possibilities which should be explored.

(a)   Cut a long, narrow strip and sew one end to the fabric. Make loops of varying length and stitch at both sides of each loop.

(b)   Cut a fairly wide strip much longer than required, and stitch both ends to the fabric, leaving the edges free. Pleat or tuck the spare leather at random and stitch invisibly until all the leather lies flat. Straight strips of pliable leather can be fringed and then eased round curved lines and circles.

Fringes can be looped, pleated, and tucked up as desired, but remember to cut them extra long to allow for this. Another method is to place bugle beads under a fringe and sew it across them.

20   Here are two ideas which can be carried out with small oddments of leather.

(a)   Cut a circle of leather and on the wrong side mark eight points. At each point cut out a small triangle. Now take eight oblongs of leather, the top edges being twice the width of the space between each cut in the circle, and the sides twice the length of the top. Fringe these pieces to within 6 mm ($\frac{1}{4}$ in.) of the top, cutting them into eight lengths. Sew the corners of the fringed leather to the corners of the cuts. Push the spare leather into a pleat in the middle and stitch on each side of it. Stitch the ends of the four outer fringes and leave the middle four loose.

(b)   Stick or stitch a curtain ring or a button to a background. Cut a circle of leather slightly larger than the ring and sew it in place. If desired punch a hole in the middle of the leather, and put a piece of Indian mirror glass in the centre of the ring. Sew the leather in place. Pipe the edge of the leather with a 6 mm ($\frac{1}{4}$ in.) strip of very pliable leather. Stitch the inner edge of the strip round the circle, and neatly sew the ends of the strip together. Now push the outer edge of the strip as close to the inner one as possible and stitch it firmly.

All the ideas suggested in this chapter are capable of being developed much further, and they all have so many practical uses that it would be tedious to mention them. It remains for those who enjoy experimental work to discover these possibilities for themselves.

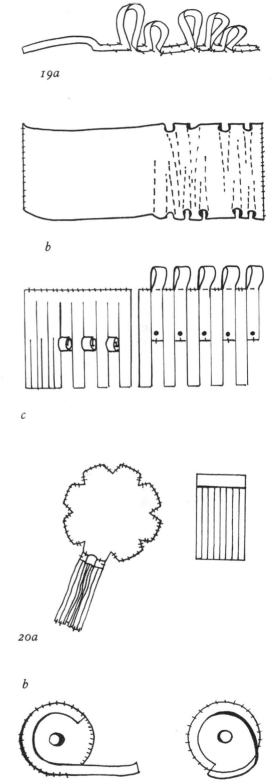

19a

b

c

20a

b

4 Inspiration from unusual objects

To the embroiderer with a lively mind, practically any object which might be regarded by other people as worthless rubbish, becomes a source of delight and inspiration. She looks upon kitchen and factory waste with a discerning eye, noting beauty of line, colour, texture and shape. She combs markets, shops, builders' dumps, zoos, fields and the seashore in an endless search for unusual articles to add to her rich store of treasures. Naturally the home is the best place to begin her search, and in the kitchen there is much to arrest her attention. Bones of all kinds simply ask to be saved for future use.

1   Oxtail bones and the spinal bones of smaller animals should be boiled and scrubbed. They are easy to use because there is a convenient hole right through most of them. See Dorothy Bramley's *Full Fathom Five*, in which bones and string were elegantly combined.

2   Small bones, particularly the wish bones of poultry are interesting. Boiled and scrubbed, they are beautiful in their natural state, but they may be varnished, sprayed or painted before use.

3   Fish bones usually should not be taken from oily fish. Cod bones are particularly beautiful, whether they are taken from the spine, fins or shoulders. They should be simmered gently and all the flesh removed, and bleached in a mild solution of *Domestos*. Fish bones are both sharp and slippery, and some are extremely fragile, so they should be handled with care. Fix them in position firmly with invisible thread before any embroidery is added. See *Underwater Ballet* by Olga Catterson page 18 and *Jar* by Jennifer Hutton page 25. Jennifer used the backbone of a fish and embroidered it.

Bones have many uses. Wired and beaded they make interesting costume jewellery, they can be applied to lampshades, and they can be embroidered and set in clear resin and used as paper weights and lamp bases.

4   Drinking straws make good padding for stitches, and as the ends can be flattened easily there is no difficulty at the beginning and ending. They can be cut into long lengths and threaded like bugles, or cut into 6 mm and 12 mm ($\frac{1}{4}$ in. and $\frac{1}{2}$ in.) lengths and sewn upright with a stitch on either side which passes through the centre.

5   Feathers are beautiful, in whole or part, and have been used for hundreds of years in embroidery. Tiny feathers

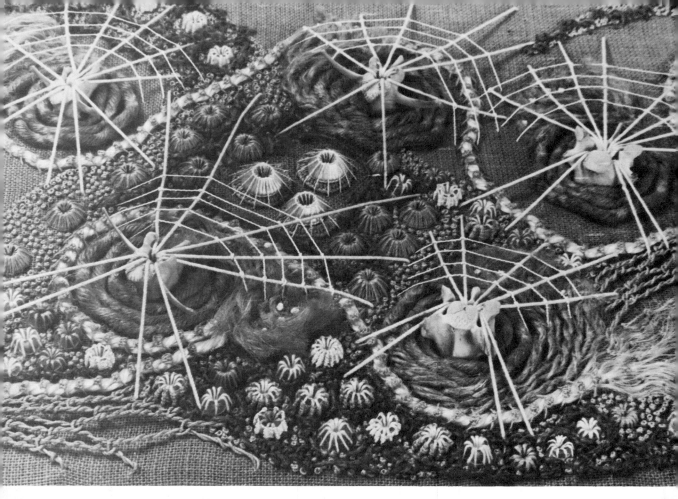

'Full Fathom Five' by Dorothy Bramley

from canaries, budgerigars and parrots are easy to stitch invisibly if the end of the quill is turned over to make a little loop. Whole or part feathers may be stuck, with care, or sewn with invisible thread. Feathers from peacocks, cockerels, pheasants, and any colourful large bird are useful adjuncts for panels, dress decoration, theatrical costume and embroidered sculpture.

6   Strips of orange peel, dried on cooking foil in an airing cupboard shrivel into lovely shapes. Varnished or left plain, they have many uses in embroidery.

7   Carefully dried vegetables such as carrots, parsnips and sweet potato have an appearance similar to semi-precious stones. Cut medium slices from the vegetables, impale them fairly well spaced on a long skewer or a knitting needle, place them on a sheet of kitchen foil and dry slowly in an airing cupboard, or on a radiator, until they are quite hard. Turn regularly and twist them round on the skewer to keep the holes open. If desired little notches may be cut in the edges of the vegetables before drying, and small cubes and sticks of the vegetables may be dried too. When

everything is quite hard, either leave them in their natural state or coat with clear varnish. The uses for these man made gems are endless. Sew on cloth as jewels, set in clear resin for paper weights, use them for jewellery combined with suffolk puff patchwork and use them in conjunction with embroidery and wire for mobiles.

8   Corks make light and pleasant padding, and look most interesting when semi-transparent fabric is draped over them. Stitch the drapery with invisible thread to hold it in place. Cover them with opaque fabric and use them for building up three dimensional embroideries. Since corks are soft it is easy to cut them into a variety of interesting shapes. See *Foreshore* page 17.

9   Egg boxes, cut apart, provide lovely little paddings or compartments for embroidery. Either cover them with cloth and line with coloured foil, for use as free standing work, or cover the outside only with cloth and stitch them on a background to give texture. Stitch them behind holes cut in a background, and bring embroidery up from their bases to spill over the surfaces.

10   Cooking foil has such a reflective surface that its uses are endless. Before mounting embroidery which has been worked on loosely woven fabric, or in which holes of some kind have been made, cover the card with foil. The effect, especially when light shines on the work, is quite dramatic. Twisted into lengths foil becomes quite strong, and it can be couched with any kind of thread. Cut it into shapes and lightly stick them to a background. With care one can sew through foil.

11   Pasta, pickling spice and seeds of all kinds from the kitchen cupboard can be stuck to work quite easily with *marvin medium*. Brush the medium on the fabric, press the pasta or seeds in position, and gently brush slightly diluted marvin over them, and leave to dry.

Leave the kitchen for a moment, and investigate the bathroom. Many interesting items lurk on shelves and in cupboards, and perhaps the best one is the loofah.

12   Loofah can be cut easily with a knife or scissors. It is possible to mould damp pieces into unusual shapes which are retained as the loofah dries. Beading and french knots, herringbone and cretan stitch marry happily with this apparently impossible object. Its lightness makes it ideal for appliqué, and its linear structure suggests a variety of possibilities with needleweaving and lacy buttonhole. It has been used successfully on lampshades, for costume jewellery, and combined with dried vegetables and set in clear resin. Lamp bases, handles for cutlery and numerous other household articles, all intensely practical, can be made with resin and loofah.

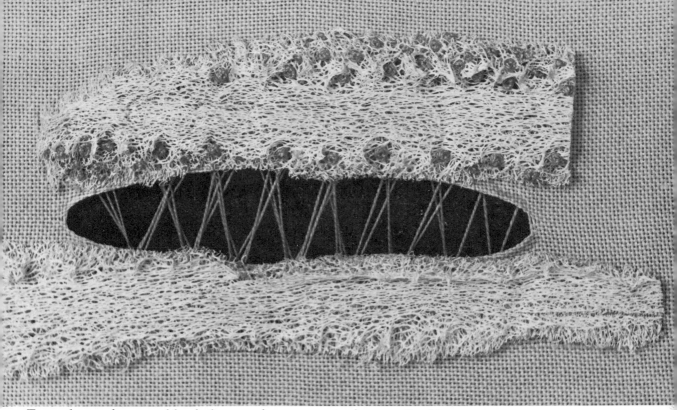

Loofah

Every house has a cubby hole or a drawer or two into which all the handyman's spare bits and pieces are tossed to await their day when they will again be useful. Many of these pieces are of great interest, and only need cleaning to render them perfectly suitable for embroidery.

13   Most kinds of wire have possibilities. Fine brass and copper wire. *Flower Piece* page 70, shows a very differ- the coloured lengths from pieces of thick flex have dozens of uses. Actually it is not so very dashing to employ wire in embroidery, as it has been used for centuries in one form or another. Most wire can be used for finger embroidery, but a needle is sometimes an asset. Look at the *Lampshade* by Pat Byrne, it was worked in buttonhole stitch with copper wire. *Flowers* by Pat Claybourne shows a very different treatment. Thick but pliable wire was wrapped with woollen and mercerised yarns, then shaped into flower like spirals. These spirals were first caught invisibly to the background, and then linked with overlapping rows of cretan and buttonhole stitch. To thread beads on wire twist one end of the wire into a knot and pass the other end through a framed background, leaving the knot on the back of it. Thread beads as desired and then take the end of the wire to the back of the work. Endless variations can be produced as most wire is strong enough to hold a shape without difficulty.

Wire can be wrapped with thread and formed into little petal and leaf shapes, which are then filled with a lacy

69

'Flower Piece' by Pay Claybourne
Hanging by Dorothy Bramley

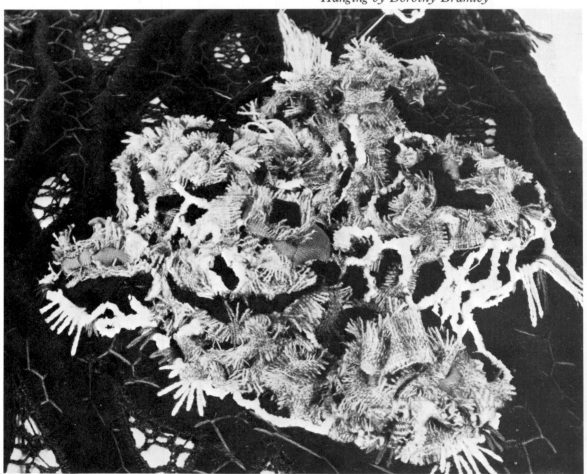

buttonhole stitch. The petals when finished are then attached to a background, and look pretty on costume and other things. This method was used in sixteenth and seventeenth century embroideries.

14 Wire netting, even though it is difficult to accept the fact, is most useful, especially for disposable and/or free standing work. It should be painted or sprayed to prevent rusting. Use it as a background for canvas type work, and stitch with the fingers or a needle with torn strips of cloth frayed at the edges, strips of felt, thick chenille, weaving yarns, string, wire, rug wool and strips of bonded fabric. Mould the netting into fantastic or naturalistic shapes before embroidering it. Hollows can be filled in with macramé, worked to fall in masses from the centre. It is possible to mould wire netting to most unusual lampshades which need only be lightly worked, or made to sparkle with pieces of cinemoid cut into strips and threaded through the mesh. Easy to make and move stage scenery, especially for out of door effects, is one more idea, and it follows that some kinds of theatrical clothing could be modelled too. The sharp ends should be carefully turned over with pliers, and pieces assembled into the shapes desired by joining them with fine wire. Large beads of all kinds, sequins, buttons, feathers and most other decoration should be wired into position. See *Hanging* by Dorothy Bramley. The domed shapes were made of moulded wire netting which were embroidered and stitched upon a heavy background.

15 Eyelets, the very large brass ones which are used for leather shopping bags and camping equipment, when covered with buttonhole or whipping are regularly used for texturing areas of embroidery. They may be used either way up, and piled upon each other, or used as a starting point for bead or other embroidery which can be suspended over them or worked through them.

16 Plastic tubing which can be bought in a variety of widths from ironmongers has many uses. It can be buttonholed on itself, almost like a piece of knitting, to make free standing work or for appliqué. Any tubing can be cut into short lengths and used as padding for stitches, or cut into longer lengths and threaded on coloured yarn and used as outsize bugles. Longer lengths used for couching may be filled with broken or whole beads before they are sewn down. To couch tubing first fix it in place with strong couching stitches of sewing cotton, then embroider a case round it with lacy buttonhole, herringbone, cretan or any other suitable stitch. Clip away the cotton stitches when the work is finished. See *Ring of Bright Water*.

17 Rubber rings and plastic, fibre or nylon washers have

Overleaf left
'*Ring of Bright Water*' by Edith John

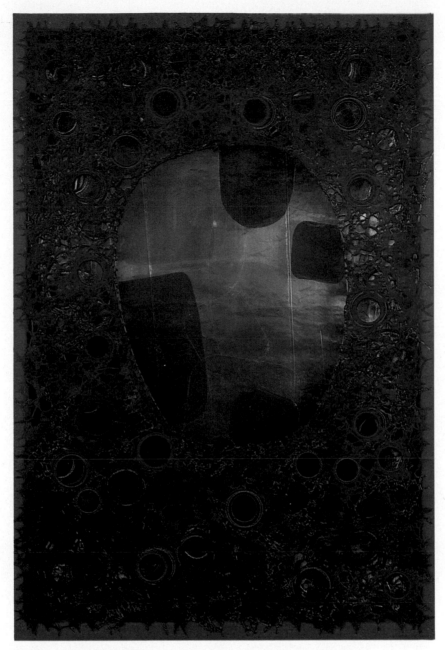

'*Between Planets*' *by Margaret Stephens. Cinemoid and embroidery*
without a background

'Exotic Plant' by Edith John. Soft and hard sculpture made to fit inside a perspex dome

much to offer. Small rings can be sewn to the ground with overcasting. To obtain a modern broderie anglaise effect, first stick small rings to the ground, then with a stiletto pierce a hole in the centre of them. Whip round, taking the thread down through the hole and up on the outside of the ring. See photographs. Large rings may be used to give a new look to cut work, which is shown quite clearly in the photograph. Before embroidering stick the rings in place and stitch about four times with invisible thread, taking care not to have the thread across the back of the area which is to be cut away. Another method of using large rubber rings is to wrap them with yarn and press them into position in rising curves. Fix with a few invisible stitches and then add the embroidery. See photograph. Soft rings can be cut and joined with *sellotape* to make larger or smaller shapes, or left open if long lines instead of circles are required.

Holes based on curtain rings 1
Holes based on curtain rings 2

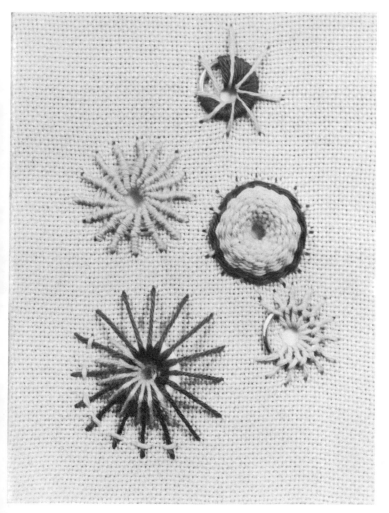

Rubber washers used for cutwork and raised work
Rota cane used as a padding

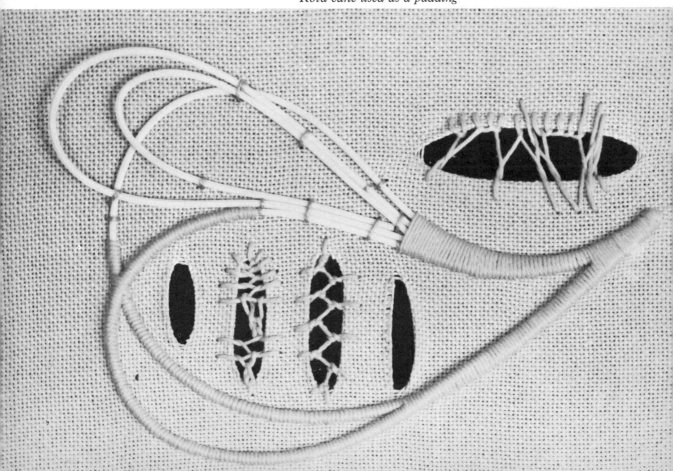

18　Ceramic tiles with decorative holes in the centre can be embroidered with Rota cane. This cane does not require damping, and it should be worked with the fingers. Large glass or wooden beads may be threaded on as the work progresses. Lacy buttonhole stitches are useful for this kind of work. The ends of the cane should be tied and glued to the back of the tile. See photograph.

19　Card or plastic cylinders from the centre of balls of embroidery and knitting yarns can be wrapped with lengths of cloth or yarn, or covered with leather and used in all manner of embroideries. In *Surfside* the card shapes were used to represent the foamy edge of a wave page 76.

20　Vacuum formed shapes of clear acetate are often used for packing material. The dome shaped ones with a lip are a joy to use. They may be placed over piled up beads and invisibly stitched into position as in *Ring of Bright Water,* or joined in pairs to make spheres filled with embroidery for mobiles. The domes are useful too for the tops of paperweights. Where vacuum forming equipment is available, make transparent shapes over beaded and other firmly raised work. These shapes can be used as a permanent cover to protect work if the spare acetate is cut away and the edges stuck down with *marvin medium.* They have been used for finger plates, burses, and boxes. The colour of the embroidery is muted, but an interesting wet look is an added attraction. These plastic covers are beautiful in themselves, and spare ones should be used in appliqué.

21　Nails, tin-tacks and screws stitched in masses with waxed thread make interesting textures, and their natural colour is pleasing, but those who wish to disguise these common objects often spray them with paint. A firm strong background is necessary and it should be strengthened with iron-on *vilene.*

22　Polythene sheeting, and bags and sacks which come in pearly white, black and cinnamon colour, are a joy to use. They can be machined, or hand sewn, and heat sealed with the tip of a warm iron. Thin sheeting made up into little bags of various shapes and stuffed with coloured fabric, foil or tissue paper, can be made into flower or other shapes when arranged on a background and caught down along one edge or at a corner. Cut sheets or bags into strips and use them as embroidery threads. Plait them, make them into cords, and work them as macramé. Use pieces either ruched or flat for appliqué, especially over other embroidery to tone down colour. Polythene sacks and covers in which carpets are delivered are woven from narrow strips of polythene. They can be embroidered most effectively with their own threads and look especially convincing with pulled work. See page 86. Zigzag machining

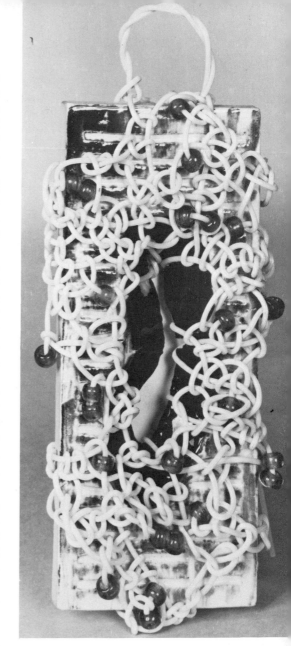

Ceramic tile

75

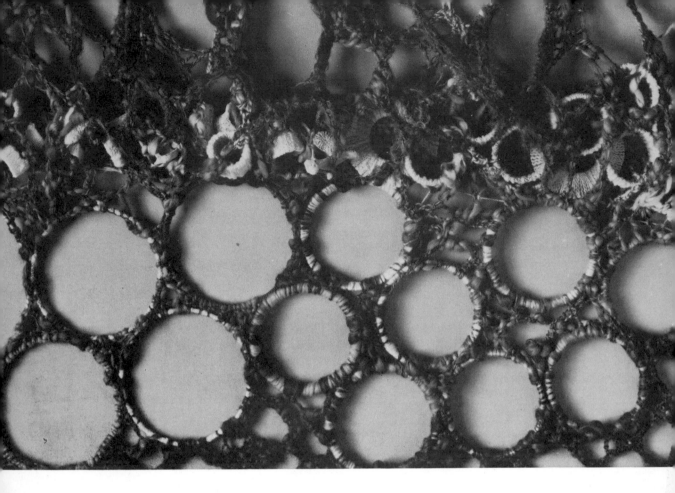

'Surfside' by Edith John

can be worked on this woven polythene. It makes good place mats, lampshades, bags, hats and many other articles for domestic use.

23 Wood shavings should be gathered up quickly before they are swept into the dustbin. Their beauty of form, colour and texture are a delight to the eye. Use them for texturing surfaces, and stick or stitch them in place. Wooden beads, bones, seeds, string and washers make good companions for wood shavings.

24 Paper in any form. Newspaper, tissue, sheets from magazines, old greetings cards, corrugated paper and kitchen paper can be utilized in embroidery. Pasted with *polycell* or *marvin medium* in layers, it becomes strong and durable, and it will take embroidery if little holes are first pierced in it with a stiletto. Interesting news items can be preserved for ever and made into family heirlooms, on such things as panels, trays, lampshades, book covers and finger plates. The stitchery must be discreet and carefully chosen, and black work is one method which looks good with newsprint. Alternatively look on paper as useful for disposable embroidery, as mentioned in the section on lampshades. One embroiderer incorporated torn strips of

newspaper into a piece of shadow work on organdie and the result was arresting. Paper embroidery is far from new. In the eighteenth century in France nuns worked with floss silk on brown paper, and in Victorian times book marks and other items were worked with silk on perforated card.

25 Peg board makes a good background for embroidery, either for children or for the mature and experienced needlewoman'

26 Clear and coloured acetate sheeting can be used in numerous ways. It makes an interesting background and if embroidered on the wrong side a modern approach to shadow work is the result. Use a large needle, and with care even textured threads such as Twilley's *bubble cotton* can be used. Keep the stitches fairly large and do not sew too near the edge. Young people have managed to make angels and kings, free standing, by this method. Sequins can be stuck on with *marvin medium*. If a bubbly surface is needed spread a thin layer of clear *bostik* No.1 over it. For interesting effects of depth and tone, apply shapes of coloured acetate over areas of flattish embroidery with invisible thread. Keep the stitches well spaced and fairly long. Acetate can be pleated, rolled and twisted and attached to a background with the fewest possible invisible stitches. Look at the curled top of the water in *The Wave* page 19. Although the acetate is attached so lightly it is firm enough to support the white embroidery. Torn strips with irregular edges can be arranged on top of finished work, as in *Underwater Ballet* by Olga Catterson page 18. Embroideries which have no background are enhanced if strips or shapes of coloured acetate are fixed at the back of the work. The most fascinating method of all, which gives an unbelievable depth and luminosity to work, was evolved by Margaret Stephens in *Between Planets*, facing page 72. Briefly the method she used was as follows:

1 Cover a deep frame but do not add a background.

2 Across the back of the frame sew some foundation threads of invisible fishing line.

3 Assemble a collage of pieces of coloured acetate and stitch the pieces together with invisible thread.

4 Place the collage on top of the foundation threads and stitch it in place invisibly.

5 Surround the collage with a filling of lacy buttonhole and covered curtain rings.

6 Stretch transparent foundation threads across the top of the frame.

7 Work lace buttonhole and covered rings on and between these threads, leaving the central area unworked.

8 A piece of hardboard covered with gold metallic paper

was nailed behind the work to act as a reflective background.

27 Sometimes scraps of metal turnings, all fluted and curled can be discovered in odd corners. They are generally dirty and greasy, but if they are washed carefully and dried in an oven, their beauty becomes apparent. The metal is sharp and should be treated with care. Fix it on a strong, possibly backed, fabric such as bonded tweedy material, vinyl, or leather, with fine wire. A little *marvin medium* trailed over it will help to smooth the edges and prevent rusting. Embroidery should be discreet. Large beads, washers, sequin waste, leather appliqué and wire stitchery all look right with metallic strips.

28 Clear *bostik* No. 1 can be used as an embroidery thread, and it is most effective in small areas under glass, for such decorative objects as paper weights. Embroider in a crusty manner with beads and sequins or other raised work, then with great care and a steady hand squeeze the thinnest trickle of *bostik* possible from one raised piece to another, so that the trail of glue is actually suspended across a space. Make a very open spider web and leave it to dry. The finished effect is lovely, especially under a magnifying dome, and the work is surprisingly strong. Clear *bostik* will stick cinemoid, but it eats into it and gives a bubbly surface. When interestingly textured pieces of cinemoid are required, smear them lightly all over with clear *bostik*.

29 *Marvin medium* is a great asset to the needlewomen. For sealing costume jewellery like beaded brooches, finish and mount the work, then brush it over carefully with full strength *marvin medium*. Although milky and opaque when in a liquid state it dries hard and clear, giving a jewel like polish to the work and protecting it from dust and dirt. *Marvin medium* is equally useful for sealing tarnishable metal threads, and it is always brushed over finished work. It prevents fraying, and it will stick anything to anything, therefore for theatrical costume especially it is a great time and cost saver, as sequins and beads can be stuck in position very quickly indeed, and there is surely no reason why seams should not be stuck? Many people make paper weights, using glass tops which are heavy and difficult to fix over embroidery in a professional looking manner. Paint *marvin medium* full strength fairly thickly over the mounted embroidery, then press the glass top in position. The *marvin medium* will probably take a week or two to dry out, but it will grip the top securely, and as it clears it will make shiny images which are quite attractive. Use *marvin medium* to stick pieces of cinemoid together and to fix semi-precious stones to elaborate work.

5 Manipulating stitches

We are often told that to teach techniques is to stifle creativity, yet it does not appear to be logical to state that one proposes to experiment with stitches if one knows precisely nothing about them. It is agreed that those who devote too much time to studying traditional forms of stitchery become so involved with technique that it is very difficult to persuade them that invention is both possible and desirable, and that technique is not necessarily lost in the process. Indeed it is the really skilful needlewoman who appears to be the most afraid of departing from well worn paths, because as soon as she begins to experiment all the signposts disappear and she feels confused. Is she doing the right thing? Will someone pour scorn on her efforts and pronounce them to be wrong, to be lower than her usual high standard of meticulous workmanship? At the same time she admires sincerely good examples of experimental stitchery, and longs to achieve something which is entirely her own creation.

Therefore this chapter has been devised in an attempt to help all those who wish to experiment, whether they have a great deal of skill and knowledge, or none at all.

For convenience stitches are placed in family groups, and those who propose to sit for examinations in embroidery need to understand and to recognise these groups.

Group 1

(a) *Flat stitches* are made very simply, without any looping or knotting of the thread. Included among them are running stitch, herringbone and fishbone.

Herringbone variation

Buttonhole filling

(b)   *Looped stitches* are made by passing the thread under the needle before it is withdrawn from the ground. The most well known of these stitches are all the varieties of buttonhole, feather and cretan stitch.

(c)   *Chained stitches* are numerous, and in all of them there is a closed unit like a link in a chain. Wheatear, rope stitch and crested chain are good examples.

Chained wheatear

Long-armed double knot

(d)   *Knotted stitches* are either complete in themselves like French knots and bullion knots, or else a knot is made during the working of a stitch. Knotted buttonhole, knotted chain, double knot and knotted fly stitch show the latter technique.

(e)   *Composite stitches* are composed of two or more separate stages, the first of which must be completed before the second one is begun. The second stage is finished and then if there is a third or even a fourth stage, they are each completed in their turn. All whipped stitches, threaded stitches, raised stem, guilloche stitch and interlacing stitch are fair examples.

Threaded run stitch variation

(f) *Lace stitches* as the name suggests do not pass through the ground except at the edges of the shapes in which they are worked. Needlepoint lace, lacy buttonhole, surface darning, surface needleweaving, and honeycomb are all lace stitches.

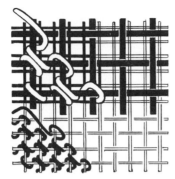

Double twisted lattice

The diagrams show the relative positions of needle and thread for each group of stitches.

Group 2 includes all the stitches which are associated with particular methods, such as canvas work, drawn ground and drawn thread work. For instance florentine, smyrna cross and plait stitch are canvas stitches: and wave stitch, cobbler stitch and diagonal chevron are drawn ground stitches. It should be noted that all the stitches in Group 2 fall into one of the sections of Group 1.

Group 3 leads to the uses of stitches.
(a) Line or outline stitches are narrow, like stem, double knot and chain stitch.
(b) Border or band stitches as the name suggests are broader than line stitches, and four well known ones are herringbone, guilloche, chevron and satin stitch.
(c) *Filling stitches* are divided into three groups:
   1 *Closed or solid fillings,* which cover the ground completely, ie, long and short, surface darning, satin stitch and most canvas stitches.
   2 *Open fillings* are lace-like and the ground can be seen through them. All couched fillings, most lace fillings, darnings and drawn ground fillings fall into this category.
   3 *Powdered fillings* are dotted over an area, and among these are seeding, fly stitch, link stitch and french knots.
(d) *Shading stitches.* The best known shading stitches are long and short, florentine and satin stitch. The Chinese excelled at satin stitch and used it for shading in three different ways:

Manipulating buttonhole by Anne Lees

◀ *Experimental herringbone by Marion Baxter*

1 Closed bands.

2 Voided. In this method a microscopic line of fabric is left between each band of satin stitch.

3 Encroached. Each row of satin stitches is interlocked a fraction with the preceding one.

Apart from using gradation of tone to achieve shading there are other more subtle methods which are often overlooked.

1 Change the direction of the stitch. This is a particularly good idea when floss silk or mercerised thread is being used. The simplest way to change the direction is to fill a circle spirally with stem or chain stitch worked very closely.

2 Change the thread gradually from thin to very thick and do not change the colour.

3 Using the same thread gradually alter the tone by working stitches very close together and then opening them out. French knots, seeding, buttonhole fillings and herringbone give good results.

4 Without changing either thread or colour alter the size of stitches, beginning quite small and ending long. Chain and alternating stem are examples.

5 In couched fillings forget the old rule about keeping the threads the same distance apart. Pack some threads close together and open others considerably.

Group 4 Surface stitchery lies mainly on the top of the fabric, and very little of the thread is to be seen on the underside of the work. Lace fillings, many line and band stitches, and couched fillings, come into this group.

Obviously we cannot leave stitches in these closed compartments. The first thing one must realise is that line and band stitches can be used as filling and shading stitches, and that most canvas stitches turn into drawn ground if they are worked fairly tightly on loosely woven fabric. Most stitches can be worked on canvas, or on transparent fabric as shadow work, and they can be worked freely or on the counted thread. It follows that these groups which we have been discussing are for guidance only. Experienced embroiderers do not need to accept any particular grouping unless there is a specific reason for doing so.

Do not spend too much time copying stitches from books, as it is very limiting. Remember that it is quite impossible for an author to suggest all the uses for, and variations of, every stitch and filling. Stitch drawings may be misleading too, as they must be opened out in order to show the working method clearly. The most inhibiting effect comes from the fact that nearly all stitch drawings are shown on a neat straight line, with each stitch exactly the same size as its neighbour. However if one varies the size and direction of

Facing page
Interesting threads change
the character of stitches

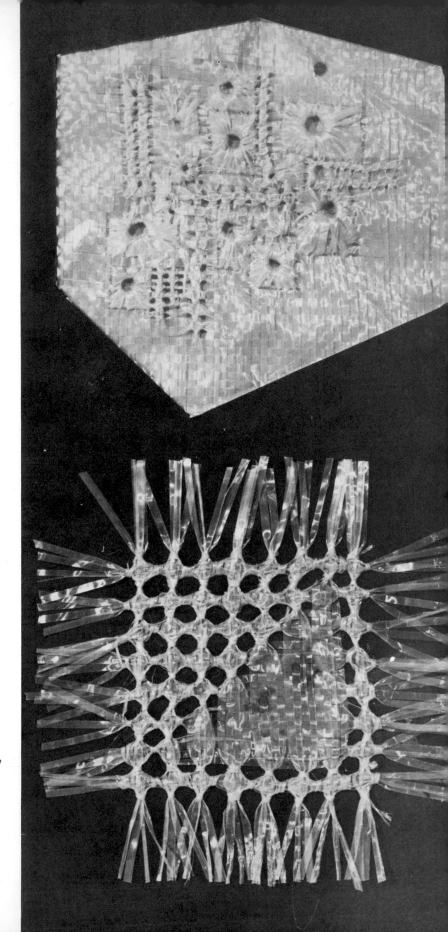

Polythene sack embroidery
by Mary Paulucy

Facing page
'Amaryllis' by Dorothy
Petty Piled chain stitch

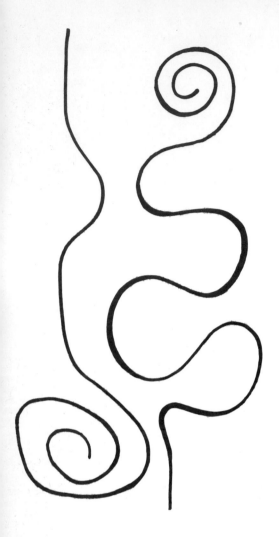

Lines which suggest plant growth for experimental stitchery

stitches in a controlled manner, much more impact will be obtained. There is a wide spread feeling that once a line of stitches has been worked, that is the end of it, but if stitches are heaped in rows, or separately upon each other, a sculptured effect is achieved easily and no padding is required.

The character of every stitch can be altered considerably by using knobbly, hairy and other textured yarns. This adds spice to examination questions about the stitches we would use to obtain a smooth or a rough effect. Satin stitch, for instance, is deliciously smooth when executed with floss silk, but very uneven when worked with knobbly cotton.

The size of the stitch depends on the effect one wishes to obtain and/or the thickness of the thread. Normally one would work quite a small stitch with a thin thread and a long one with a thick thread, but one does not always wish to be normal.

Stitches and threads require needles. Many embroiderers imagine that the best sewing is done with a needle so fine that it strains the sight to thread it. This is not true. A needle should be large enough to take the thread easily through the ground, as far less damage is done to the thread and to the fabric if one does not have to tug. Floss silk threads require a large eyed needle, and really thick or textured threads require the largest chenille needles and perhaps some help from a stiletto too.

Another theory which is patently false is that fine embroidery is good embroidery. Very fine stitchery often hides a multitude of faults, and it takes a really skilful needlewoman to embroider perfectly with rope like threads. It cannot be denied that good fine work is breathtaking, but those whose sight is becoming weaker are still capable of producing first class work on a large scale.

Time and size are two important factors in favour of coarse embroidery, especially when one is executing commissions. It seems logical to produce large scale stitchery on large pieces of work, especially when only a short time is allowed for completion. From this point it is necessary to embark on a voyage of discovery. On a piece of fabric draw two simple curved lines which suggest plant growth. Take a length of thick cotton and choose a border stitch such as herringbone, and work the first line. It will be found that on an outer curve the stitch must be widened, and contracted on an inner curve. Some stitches change out of all recognition when worked on a curve, and perhaps the most interesting results are obtained with surprise chain.

Use thick cotton for the second line, and change the stitch very often, in order to alter the thickness of it. Begin with running stitch, then in turn change to back stitch, stem stitch, rope, feather, cretan and so on. It will be dis-

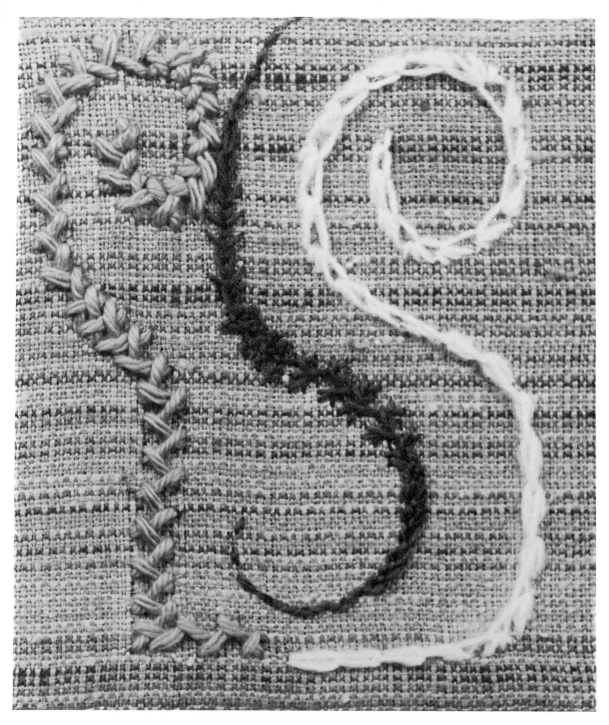

Stitches worked on a curve give interesting results

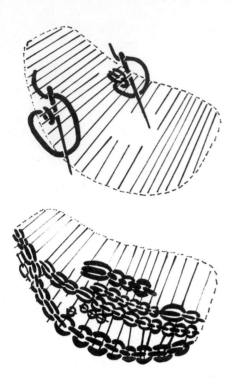

Raised chain band used as a filling stitch
(a) Place threads for grounding irregularly
(b) Work on them with different weights of thread

covered that there is quite an art in moving smoothly from one stitch to another without an obvious break. Another experiment requires only one stitch, but a change of thread from very fine to quite thick as the work progresses along a line.

From simple experiments move to something more difficult. Choose one stitch, such as vandyke or sheaf stitch, and sylko perlé No. 5. Work several centimetres/ inches of the stitch until it is really committed to memory, then begin again. Deliberately omit one movement, or repeat a movement twice, or even three times. Re-arrange the working order. Use bugles instead of padding, especially for stitches such as raised chain band or sheaf. Work in a circle, work back on top of the stitch and go backwards and forwards alternately. Cut holes in the cloth and work the stitch over the holes. Try to carry out a whole stitch by threading several small beads on the needle for each part of it, so that the thread can be seen only on the back of the work. Suddenly something quite new will be evolved, but the new stitch must be a variation of that which one started with. It is too easy to 'discover' a very well known stitch which is not the one which was chosen in the beginning. See photograph of experiments with herringbone, buttonhole and vandyke stitches.

Surprises are in store. One person decided to experiment with braid stitch, and she discovered to her amazement that it is raised chain band worked in one stage instead of two. She could move and manipulate the stitch at will by pushing it around with her needle or her fingers.

Any stitch which is worked on a ladder of satin stitch can be turned into a lovely textured filling, and raised chain band is one of the prettiest. See diagram. Arrange long bars over the shape which is to be filled, splaying them where necessary, and work rows and rows of chain stitch on them, using several different thicknesses of thread. Do not complete every line. At times pick up two or more of the foundation threads, and occasionally skip one. This work does present problems. It should be done in a frame and there must be complete control of the foundation threads. Try to work raised chain band across a covered frame with no background, as suggested in Chapter 1, or across holes cut in the fabric.

To carry these suggestions any further would defeat our object. The embroiderer must now go forward alone and discover for herself the wonderful possibilities of experimental stitchery.

A few words about beads and sequins is necessary, since they are usually stitched to a background, and the method chosen is all too often far from interesting.

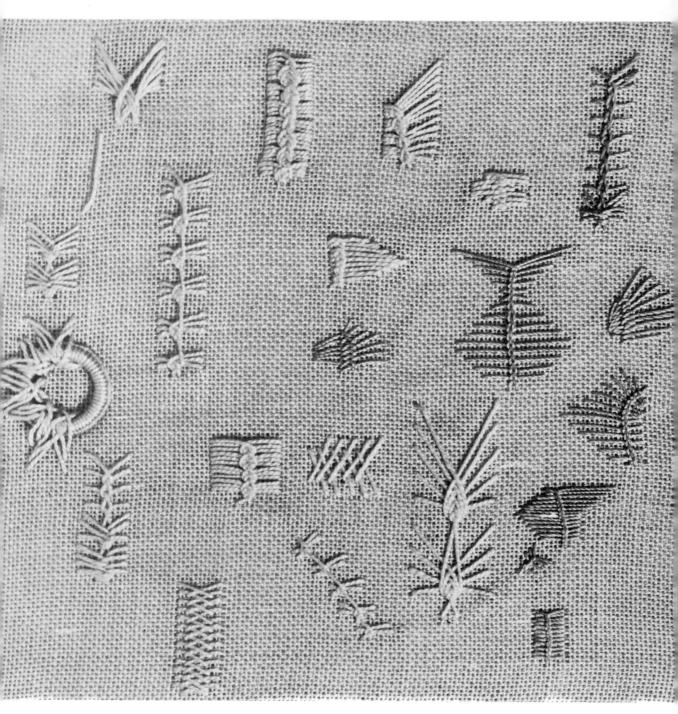

Manipulating vandyke stitch by Honor Costelloe

1 Just as stitches like french knots may be heaped upon each other, so may beads and sequins. First fill in an area with beads, and then begin again and build up unevenly until a really crusty effect is obtained.

2 Bugles may be criss-crossed one over the other.

3 Thread any kind of beads, say six at a time and stitch them down in these lengths, crossing and re-crossing in any order. The number of beads may be changed at will.

4 To achieve free standing effects put a knot on the end of a piece of fine wire, pass the other end through a framed background, and arrange beads on it to any desired height. Then, either bend the beaded piece of wire into a loop and pass its free end back through the fabric, or put an extra large bead on the top of those already there, then press the wire back through all the smaller beads and through the fabric. The wire can be ended after each operation, or if it is fairly long take it up through the fabric and use it again.

5 Thread beads on long lengths of linen or cotton or man made yarn and sew these lengths as fringes or tassels for the modern shaggy look.

6 Thread one bugle then one small round bead on a cotton, then take the needle back through the bugle. The beads will remain upright. Arrange in groups. Alternatively put several small beads above the bugle before returning the needle through it to the back of the work.

7 Thread one bugle, one sequin and one bugle, then take the needle to the back of the fabric a short distance away from the spot where it entered originally. The bugles will stand up with the sequin like a little wheel between them. Repeat, using a round bead instead of a sequin. Both of these methods give a lovely crusty appearance when they are used to fill whole areas.

Beads are expensive, and for many people they are difficult to obtain. Home made beads are wonderfully attractive, and they can be made exactly the right size and shape for any piece of work. When I was four years old my friends and I were taught to make paper beads, and the method is still in use. Two diagrams for paper patterns are shown, and the beads will be quite successful if at its widest the paper is cut any width from 13 mm ($\frac{1}{2}$ in.) to about 203 mm (8 in.). Use coloured sheets from magazines, black and white advertisements, wallpaper or any paper which will give the texture and colour required. Take a knitting needle and place it across the wide end of a strip of paper, and roll it very tightly. Use *copydex* to stick the last 50 mm (2 in.) of paper in place. When the paste is dry slip the bead off the needle. Coat with clear nail varnish if a shiny look is needed. Beads can also be made with *polyfilla*. Mix the powder according to directions, adding a colouring agent if required, and mould into beads with the fingers. Roll in a piece of wet towelling to give a smooth surface and leave to dry for two hours. Thread the beads on fine knitting needles, and support the needles across bobbins or some other firm base, and leave to dry for two days. Remove the needles and clean the holes with a sharp knife. Polish with emery paper and varnish.

Instead of mixing colour with the *polyfilla* make plain beads, and when they are dry score patterns or paint patterns on them, then varnish if necessary.

It follows that flat shapes of *polyfilla* dried on a knitting needle make attractive additions to embroidery. So do paper shapes made by pasting several layers of paper together and paring them to a good shape when dry. Varnish if necessary.

To make log beads, take a piece of thin and narrow cardboard tubing, a jumbo sized straw, or a firm roll made by pasting paper into a narrow tube, and cut into pieces of any desired length. Take a long length of fine string, or wool, or mercerised embroidery thread, and stick the end inside the piece of tube. Roll the thread closely round the tube, pasting it at the top and bottom only. Glue the remaining end inside the tube. Varnish or paste over with *marvin medium*.

To make cloth beads, cut the cloth to the patterns given above for paper beads. Take a length of drinking straw about 76 mm (3 in.) wider than the cloth and paste it in the centre to the width of the cloth. Place the cloth face downwards on a table, and beginning at the wide end roll it round the straw. Stick the last 50–76 mm (2 or 3 in.). Paste over the bead with *marvin medium* if a wet look is required, or coat with *polycell*. When the bead is hard and dry cut off the exposed ends of the straw.

8   Take any shape or size of flat sequins except perhaps the smallest, and fold them down the middle so that one half stands at a right angle to the other. Arrange them back to back, or in any other manner which suggests itself, and sew them down either with stitches or beads.

9   Take large oval and round sequins and roll them into tubes. Stitch over them to hold the shape and once into the holes in the sequins.

10   Cut large oval or round sequins spirally to the centre. This results in springs which can be pulled open in a variety of interesting ways.

11   Make hanging motifs for costume and panels by alternating large flat sequins on a thread with groups of small beads.

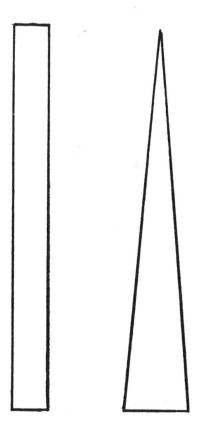

Two patterns for paper beads

12 Fold large sequins concertina fashion.

13 Take dome shaped sequins and sew them in pairs face to face and back to back.

14 Take large sequins and fold upwards two flaps, one on each side, leaving a flat area in the middle.

The following ideas are for large oval sequins.

15 Make a fold lengthwise from the tip to half way up the sequin. This gives a petal shape.

16 Fold diagonally at right angles.

17 Roll end to end and sew the ends together. Hang a little bead tassel through it.

18 Cockscomb. Cut as shown in the diagram and fold alternate pieces forwards and backwards.

19 Bud. Cut as shown and fold the side pieces upwards as shown by the dotted line.

20 Cut as shown and fold alternate pieces upwards on the dotted lines.

21 Spiral. Cut as shown and sew the ends tightly together.

22 Flower. Cut as shown. Fold the outer pieces forwards and the inner pieces backwards. Leave the two centre pieces flat.

23 Signpost. Cut as shown and fold alternate pieces backwards and forwards.

There are countless ways of arranging folded and cut sequins, and each embroiderer will discover her own methods. It will be found that all the ideas suggested above enhance the reflective qualities of sequins. Use waxed thread, as the cut edges are sometimes rather sharp, and strengthen the background with iron-on *vilene* or any other suitable fabric. Remember that the sharp ends of wire can damage fabric. Turn them firmly over, and push a tiny piece of wadding between the wire and the fabric, on the wrong side of the work.

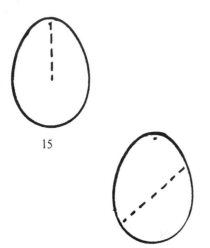

15

16

17

18

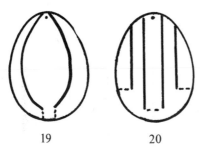

19

20

21

22

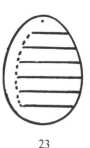

23

6 Soft and hard sculpture

Embroidery is moving quickly into the realms of sculpture, because a great deal of needlework is so highly padded that even panels have a three dimensional quality which was unheard of only a decade ago. There is some determined resistance to this kind of work, but it must be remembered that it is simply a development of traditional embroidery of hundreds of years ago. During the sixteenth century raised work of all kinds was very popular, and male costume was stuffed to such an extent that it was difficult for a man to use his sword when he was wearing a jacket. In the seventeenth century stump work, which has been described by a historian as a mock sculpture, was used for domestic and ecclesiastical work both here and on the Continent. Even when sculptured panels are found to be acceptable the large, squashy, outsize, chocolate eclairs, typewriters and radishes, which are life-like in colour and texture, call forth cries of dismay from the more traditionally minded embroiderers. Yet children love them, instantly accepting them as delightful toys, and realising what fun it is to sit on a life like cream cake which causes no damage to the clothes. So, apart from the skill, observation, and ingenuity which are needed in order to achieve soft sculpture, it is obvious that in time it will result in some unique and harmless playthings for the little ones. Teenagers like squashy furniture, which is another development of soft sculpture, and people of all ages are interested in bags and boxes which look soft and floppy outside but in which a firm interior makes a practical article.

For those who cannot be persuaded that soft sculpture is anything but a gimmick, free standing sculptured objects which are rigid often have a great appeal.

Highly padded panels make a gentle introduction to this chapter, as most embroiderers like quilting and appliqué, two traditional methods which are being developed into something quite new.

1 *Lava* by Edith John demonstrates highly padded appliqué. Large pieces of roughly cut thick foam were stitched to the background. Then on pieces of tweedy furnishing fabric the pattern shapes were marked. These were cut out with very generous turnings, and some of the edges were frayed to a depth of 25 mm (1 in.). Each piece was pinned in place round the edges, and twisted and draped and pinned over and among the pieces of foam. The

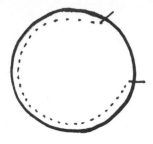

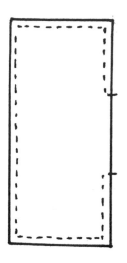

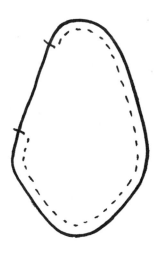

Cut two pieces for each shape. Machine 6 mm ($\frac{1}{4}$ in.) from edge. Leave opening. Turn. Stuff with kapok (not too tightly). Close opening with invisible stitches

edges were then stitched invisibly in place, and any extra fabric was tucked or pleated until a perfect fit was obtained. A large number of invisible seeding stitches were used to control the fabric as it oozed over the padding, but no stitches were taken through the foam. The central part of the design was made by sticking large rubber rings, with flat tops, upon the background and overcasting them with thick embroidery cotton. See facing page 97.

2   *Roots* by Judith Johnstone was developed by another method. The appliqué was cut much larger than necessary and a very narrow turning was pressed all round each piece. The pieces were eased and stitched a little at a time, and crumpled tissue paper was pushed under the fabric wherever a bump was required. The fabric was held over each bump with a stitch or two, and then more outlining, and more padding were added until the shapes were finished. Note how the design was taken over the edge of the frame. Large glass beads, the same colour as the fabric, were tucked into hollows for extra textural effect. Page 97.

3   *Carberry* by Edith John shows how the previous method can be taken a stage further. The trees trunks were worked exactly as *Roots,* but the branches and roots were made separately of funnel shaped pieces of fabric, which were stuffed and then embroidered before being bent into shape and attached to the work. Page 98.

4   *Sunflower* by Dorothy Petty is a very rich piece of embroidery. It was based on the seed head of a giant sunflower. The centre was made of three triangular quilted shapes, ornamented above with gold kid, gold thread and gold beads, and below with buttonholed rings in dark tones. These pieces when finished were stiff enough to be bent into shape, so that they curved away from the background. A few stitches were needed to attach them to the centre and the sides of the work. The curly leaves round the edges were made of double pieces of gold kid, which were stuffed and wired, and beaded round the edges. These leaves were held with only one or two stitches at their bases. Page 63.

5   A quicker and very effective method is to make bags of two pieces of fabric, machined together on the wrong side and turned through a small opening, stuffed lightly, and then hand stitched to close the open end. These bags can be of any shape and in many sizes, and embroidery, quilting or beading added to them as necessary. Attach them to the background by one side or end only, arranging them as an abstract, geometric or floral pattern. Covered wire, wired beads, pleated strips of fabric, and stitchery can be added to enhance the effect. Suffolk puff patchwork makes interesting bags. To work cut out circles of fabric, any

'Ring' by Olga Catterson. Embroidery on a cardboard hoop, with
crochet

'Lava' by Edith John. Embroidery on a deep frame, with sculptured padding and rubber washers

'Roots' by Judith Johnstone

*Decorate finished bags with
machine quilting, beads or hand
stitchery*

'Carberry' by Edith John

size. Turn in a fairly deep edge and gather it tightly, pulling the fabric into a fat puff with a neat hole in the middle. These puffs should be sewn individually to the background with an invisible stitch or two in the centre of the hole. From the hole hang long loops of ribbon or fabric, or wired beads, or tassels. Alternatively sew beads or sequins in the hole. Very large puffs may need a tiny stitch or two at the edges. Pretty, soft transparent fabrics make excellent suffolk puffs.

6   The traditional appliqué of the Panama Indians can be developed into sculptured forms if the right materials are used. *Method:*

Frame a piece of firm bonded fabric, with a knitted weave, and on it mark the pattern. A beginner should make a simple pattern, preferably of curved shapes, as these are easier to control. Behind this fabric tack several layers of fabric of different colours and weights, firmly woven and not liable to fray badly. These layers should be practically as large as the top piece. Tack through all the layers firmly, but do not stitch across the pattern areas. As the idea is to cut away pieces of material and expose each of the layers

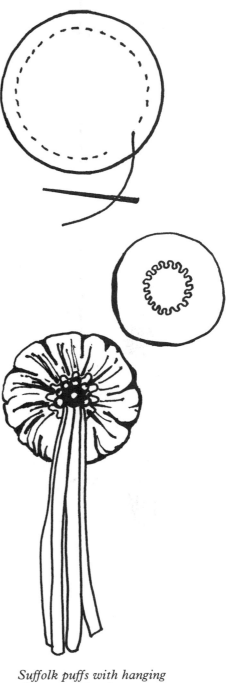

Suffolk puffs with hanging ribbons and beads

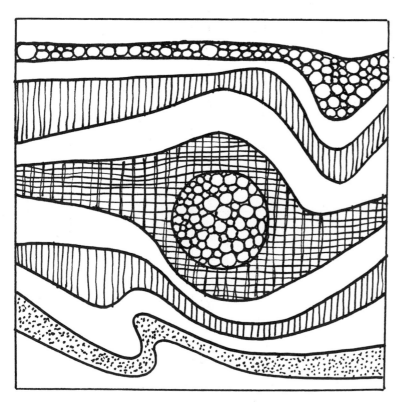

99

in a predetermined order, think carefully before embarking on the next stage. Take a small pair of sharp pointed scissors and cut away the top fabric only from one portion of the design, then turn its edge in with a needle and oversew it through all the remaining layers. Next cut away two layers in another shape, and try to pare the second one so that the edge of the first layer is easy to oversew. Proceed in this manner, gradually cutting through more layers until the pattern is complete. Pieces worked in this manner may be cut out and used as appliqué, or used as complete pieces of needlework. Add stitchery if it should be necessary.

7   Instead of using a frame, try a firm surface like chipboard. Covered with some kind of fabric it makes a good base for sculptural embroidery. See *Reflections* by Angela Lewis. A piece of chipboard was covered with silver *melinex*, (kitchen foil would have been equally effective), and then sections of a large cardboard hoop covered in the same way, were nailed to it. The top edges of these arcs were painted black, and large headed nails were tapped along these edges at 13 mm ($\frac{1}{2}$ in.) intervals, leaving about 6 mm ($\frac{1}{4}$ in.) of the nail exposed. The nail heads served as pegs round which strands of rug wool were wound, linking one arc to another. These strands were needlewoven with a variety of threads, and then the surface of the chipboard was decorated with very open black weaving and small pieces of glued appliqué.

Free standing embroidered sculpture presents different problems, the chief of which is how to construct the pattern. For those who can draw or paint there is no real problem, as drawings of the desired object can be made, showing it from every angle. Dressmakers find it easy to construct paper mock ups, and many people simply take their tools and materials and work purely from imagination. Since embroidered sculptors are creative, there is no point in giving detailed instructions, but suggestions for simple aids might inspire embroiderers to venture into another realm.

1   Wire coat hangers can be twisted into fantastic or naturalistic shapes and embedded into a firm base. Pieces of stone, or wood are solid and practical. When the shape is ready bind it with thread or fabric, add shapes of fabric firmed with *parbond* or *vilene*, or cinemoid, or simply decorate it with lacy stitchery.

2   Dowel rods and drift-wood embedded in a covered wooden base make a perfect beginning for a piece of sculpture. *Marvin medium* and tissue paper or fine cloth can be employed to make shapes or to cover the rods, and stitchery, covered washers, sequins and whatever one cares to use will complete the work.

'*Reflections*' *by Angela Lewis*

'Heart' by Eileen Phipps

Facing page
Sculpture by Olga Catterson

3 Plastic tubing, cardboard cylinders and beads, plus stitchery, combine to make very interesting sculpture. See the photograph of *Sculpture* by Olga Catterson.

4 Florists' and other wire can be bent into lovely shapes and embroidered. The wire should be embedded into a firm base. *Hearts* by Eileen Phipps shows wire treated in this way, and finished with heart shaped mobiles of felt, cinemoid and sequins. This is a very small piece, about 203 mm (8 in.) high. *Plant Form* by Eileen Phipps is even smaller and exquisitely delicate. Fairly thick wire was shaped, and covered with bluey green gauze which was whipped to the wire and embroidered finely. The whole was attached to a firm covered base decorated with closely worked french knots. Page 105.

5 With the instructions for using *marvin medium* comes a most interesting leaflet on 'Tissue Paper Techniques'. It has been proved that delicate fabrics like organdie and chiffon can be substituted for tissue paper quite successfully, and the use of these materials leads to very attractive sculpture. See *Flower Head* by Eileen Phipps. It was constructed with lengths of wire, marvin and chiffon, with added embroidery and a little silver leather mobile. The layers of chiffon were pasted to a piece of polythene as directed and left to dry. Before they were quite hard they were peeled off the polythene, moulded into gentle curves and left to set. In passing it should be mentioned that milliners and dressmakers could make use of this technique for costume accessories for very special occasions such as weddings. Page 104.

6 Strips of *perspex* or *plexiglass*, drilled with holes and warmed in an oven until they are pliable can be bent into all kinds of shapes, then set in a heavy base and linked with stitchery. See *Curved Form* by Dorothy Bramley. Page 106.

7 Flat pieces of coloured *perspex* and off cuts can be drilled and joined with wire or other embroidery, and of course warmed and twisted if need be. Most work made with several pieces of *perspex* does not need a base.

8 Patchwork is ideal for sculpture if the patches are backed with *parbond* or card. When using *parbond* cut out the shapes required and iron them to the back of the fabric, leaving ample room between them for generous turnings. For card, cut the shapes needed from the card and draw round them on the wrong side of the fabric. Cut out with good turnings. For both *parbond* and card stick the turnings back, but do not pull them absolutely tight round the edge, because it will be difficult to sew the pieces together if there is no 'give' in the fabric. Snip curved edges before sticking them down. Add embroidery at this or any other stage, and then begin to build up a shape by

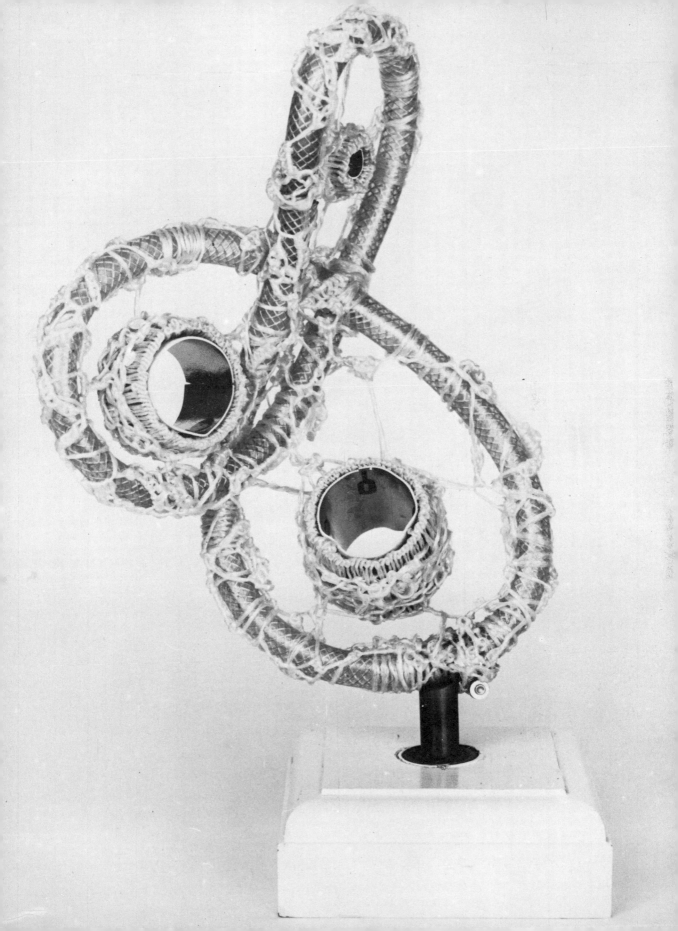

'Flower' by Eileen Phipps

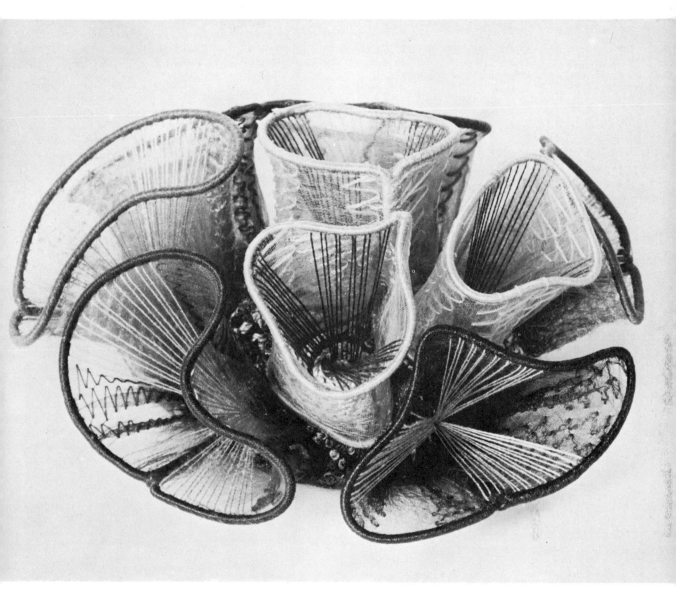

'Plant form' by Eileen Phipps
Sculpture with wire and chiffon

joining the edges with ladder stitch (see page 11) from the outside. If padding is needed stick foam to card shapes and allow for the extra thickness when cutting out the fabric. See *Architecture* by Mary Paulucy. This small piece of sculpture was inspired by the shape of a church, and it is fitted to a one inch deep covered base.

9 Polythene bags of various sizes and shapes, made by machining pieces together, or even ready made ones, can be stuffed and heat sealed and suspended from a bar. For stuffing use chopped foam, tissue paper rolled into balls, dyed wadding, wood, wool or little polystyrene shapes. Stuff some bags full, stuff others only partially and then squeeze them into interesting shapes and bind the surplus polythene with coloured cord or string. Do not rely on air alone for keeping the bags in shape, as it is sure to escape and then the whole structure will collapse.

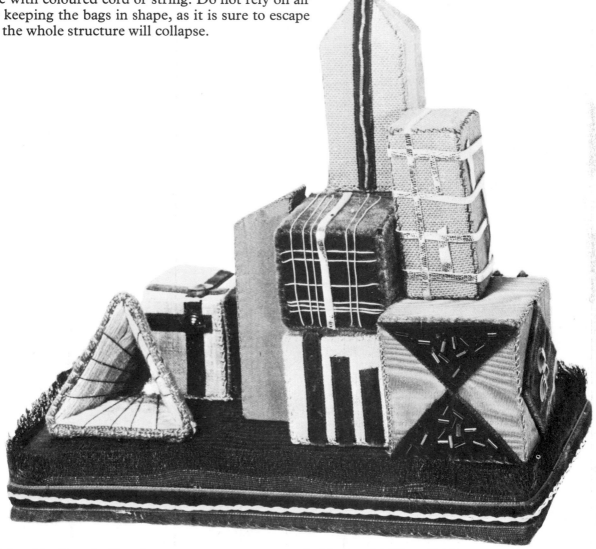

◀ *'Curved form' by Dorothy Bramley*   *Architecture by Mary Paulucy*

10 *Chocolate Eclair* by Carol Johnstone is a delicious monster about 1·2 m (4 ft) long. An eclair was studied carefully and several paintings were done from various angles. Next a mock up was made with strong paper *sellotaped* at the edges. From this pattern the amounts of fabric were estimated, and great care was taken in the choosing of them. Texture, weight and colour were most important and a search of many shops and a market was necessary before the correct materials were found. Off white crêpe was ideal for the cream, brown satin for the chocolate icing could not be improved upon, and a lightly textured fawn woollen fabric seemed to suggest the pastry. The body of the eclair was stiffened with soft canvas, and stuffed with kapok. The crêpe was machined with lines of tucking to represent the marks made by the icing nozzle and then it was sewn up and stuffed. Lacy button-hole worked with cream wool was used to represent smears of cream on the undersides of the pastry and it helped to hold the large piece of cream in place. The top of the eclair was constructed like the body, and the chocolate icing was lightly padded and stitched in place. Two embroidered hinges held the halves together.

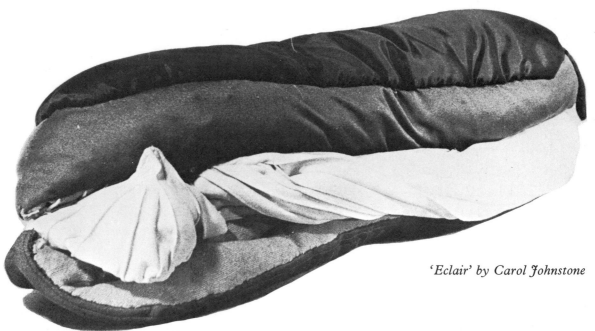

'*Eclair*' *by Carol Johnstone*

'*Lamp*' *by Kathleen Wright* ▶

11 *Lamp* by Kathleen Wright is a charming soft sculpture which began as numerous drawings and paintings of a battered old hand lamp. It was made by cutting out pieces of cloth the size of both sides, front, back, top and base with 25 mm (1 in.) turnings, and zigzag machining patches of fabric of various colours and sizes upon them. These were attached to pieces of 13 mm ($\frac{1}{2}$ in.) thick foam by the simple method of folding the turnings over it and stitching the edges invisibly. The door hinge was attached by means of a piece of cloth covered drinking straw, and the handle, though soft, was supported by two or three lengths of fine wire which were sewn inside it. The whole was lined with dark toned fabric.

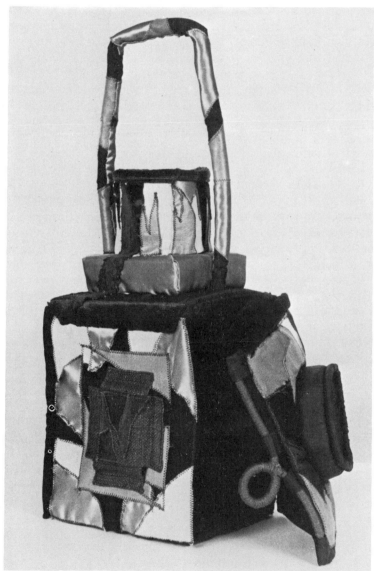

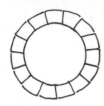

Card stuck on wrong side of leather. Leather snipped

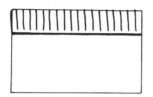

Leather folded, stuck down and fringed along the top

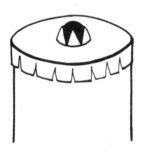

Leather stuck to edge of cylinder. Jewel in place

Completed cylinder

Facing page
'Angel' by Susan Flew

12   *Exotic Plant* combines hard and soft sculpture, collage and sewing techniques. A double piece of carpet underlay covered with fabric was used as a base, and in the centre of this a 50 mm (2 in.) deep, 203 mm (8 in.) diameter ring of card, covered with fabric, was stitched firmly. A 203 mm (8 in.) circle of thick card for the top of the ring was first padded with two wooden rings, one 152 mm (6 in.) and one 100 mm (4 in.) in diameter. Then a piece of soft gold kid with a 25 mm (1 in.) turning was stuck over this card, and it was in turn stuck on top of the ring. The edge of the leather was gathered and sewn firmly to the fabric on the ring. Whirls of weaving yarn were stuck in the hollow made by the 100 mm (4 in.) wooden ring. Next 50 mm (2 in.) high cylinders were cut from a cardboard tube, and a top of firm card was made for each one. The tops were stuck to the underside of soft leather which was cut with 13 mm ($\frac{1}{2}$ in.) turnings. These turnings were stuck to the outside of the cylinders and kept the tops in place. Each cylinder was then covered with leather which had been stuck down for 13 mm ($\frac{1}{2}$ in.) along the top and fringed. A large domed jewel embedded in a five pointed star of leather was stuck to the top of each cylinder. These were then stuck to the sides of the central ring, and held securely in place with a band of frayed fabric, which was tightly stuck round them all, like a cake frill. For extra security the frill was also stitched through the base. Between each cylinder and the centre a long oval bead was wedged and stuck, with the hole uppermost. Petal shaped bags of soft fabric were stuffed lightly and sewn in a double row round the edge. Double lengths of copper wire were stuck into each bead, and the free ends were decorated with little fringed flags of gold leather. The finished flower was stuck to a circular *perspex* base and then enclosed in a *perspex* dome, to give it the popular Victorian flavour.

It may seem incredible, but all the foregoing ideas have resulted in a new approach to embroidery for the church.
13   See *Angel* by Susan Flew. This sculpture, composed of rods of fabric in two shades of blue, is two feet tall and quite firm. Crosses and other emblems can be constructed with cardboard tubes covered with lovely fabric and richly stitched and jewelled. There is a whole field here just waiting to be explored and developed by those who would like a change from the more usual items of ecclesiastical work. These objects can be protected by spraying them with a carpet preservative such as *protasil*, and dust will then wipe off with a damp cloth. Alternatively *marvin medium* spread lightly all over will seal the work and preserve it.

Soft sculpture techniques give burses a new look.

14 Cut a 229 mm (9 in.) square of card for the top of a burse and mark a 76 mm (3 in.) circle in the centre. Pad all the outside which thick foam, tapering it along the sides of the card and round the circle. Cut out fabric, allowing 50 mm (2 in.) turnings, and stick it firmly with *copydex* to the circle. When dry stretch the rest of the fabric over the card and stick the turnings at the back. Remember to mitre the corners. Now work a piece of embroidery to fit the hollow and mount it on a piece of thin card. Stick it in place and then take a few invisible stitches through the edges of the embroidered piece to the back of the burse. Make up in the usual way.

15 Cut a 229 mm (9 in.) square of card and from the centre take out a 152 mm (6 in.) circle. Embroider the fabric cover, leaving a 152 mm (6 in.) circle empty. Stretch this over the card as shown in a diagram in Chapter 1. Embroider on another piece of fabric in a 152 mm (6 in.) circle, mount this on a 203 mm (8 in.) square of thinner card and stick it behind the hole. Make up.

16 It is possible to construct the front of a burse by interlacing 25 mm (1 in.) strips of fabric re-inforced with *parbond*, and sticking them to thin card. This method is capable of many variations and has proved successful.

17 There is no reason why soft sculpture bags should not be sewn to church embroideries such as altar frontals, pulpit falls and burses. Triangular bags made with 3 pieces of felt or bonded fabric look most effective when arranged as a crown of thorns. Doves, eagles and peacocks are most impressive when made with soft bags which overlap like feathers. They are durable and light and need very little care.

Incidentally bags are rarely damaged when stored underneath other things, they simply spring into shape as soon as they are released.

Free standing and soft sculptures have another use to which some attention might be given. In waiting rooms of hospitals, in surgeries, and in depressing areas where people have to gather and queue, they could be a talking and staring point, and a refreshing change from an illuminated tank of fishes.

Conclusion

From time immemorial people have felt the urge to express themselves, and they have searched constantly for new ways of doing so. In recent years this urge has been so great that embroidery has developed beyond the bounds of one's wildest imagining, and in many places it is now regarded as an art in its own right. Never have there been so many exhibitions of embroidery, never has it been so widely publicised, and never have there been so many groups each earnestly and eagerly vying with the other to produce a new approach. Yet in spite of all this work and publicity the word *embroidery* still suggests to many people lavender and old lace, grandmamma and cross stitch. Is this why many young people, whose lives have become a restless search for something different, tend to ignore this wonderful outlet for their creative energies? At the opposite end of Life's scale one finds ladies of eighty, young in heart and mind, eagerly accepting new ideas and developing their own.

We are told by many people that there must be an end to experimental work, that it is impossible to go on discovering new things about fabrics, threads and stitches—but has discovery in any field ever come to an end? Sometimes an idea is blocked, but usually the blockage is a warning to re-think a certain process, or a hint to open one's mind a little and accept the impossible as a challenge to one's inventive powers.

We are living in an exciting and explosive period where the arts are concerned. Never have embroiderers had such a glorious opportunity to revitalize their ancient heritage, and so, in conclusion, I would like to echo some words of Adlai Stevenson, who said 'Egg heads of the world unite. You have nothing to lose but your yolks'.

Further reading

Needleweaving, Edith John

Inspiration for Embroidery, Constance Howard

Design in Embroidery, Kathleen Whyte

Canvas Embroidery, Diana Springall

Ideas for Canvas Work, Mary Rhodes

Canvas Work, Jennifer Gray

Machine Embroidery : Technique and Design Jennifer Gray

Machine Embroidery, Gay Swift

Enjoying Embroidery, Anna Wilson

Creative Thread Design, Mair Morris

All published by B T Batsford Limited, London and
Charles T Branford Company, Newton Centre,
Massachusetts, USA

Suppliers in Great Britain

Embroidery threads and accessories, also fabrics

Mrs Mary Allen
Turnditch, Derbyshire

E J Arnold and Son Ltd
(School Suppliers)
Butterley Street
Leeds LS10 1AX

Art Needlework Industries Ltd
7 St Michael's Mansions
Ship Street
Oxford OX1 3DG

The Campden Needlecraft Centre
High Street
Chipping Campden
Gloucestershire

Craftsman's Mark Ltd
Broadlands, Shortheath
Farnham, Surrey

Dryad Ltd
Northgates
Leicester LE1 4QR

Thomas Hunter Ltd
56 Northumberland Street
Newcastle upon Tyne
NE1 7DS

John Lewis and Partners
Oxford Street
London W1

Mace and Nairn
89 Crane Street
Salisbury, Wiltshire

The Needlewoman Shop
146 Regent Street
London W1R 6BA

Nottingham Handcraft Company
(School Suppliers)
Melton Road
West Bridgford, Nottingham

Christine Riley
53 Barclay Street
Stonehaven
Kincardineshire AB3 2AR

The Silver Thimble
33 Gay Street, Bath

Mrs Joan L. Trickett
110 Marsden Road
Burnley, Lancashire

Yarns
37 High Street
Wellington TA21 8QT
Somerset

Beads and sequins

Ells and Farrier Ltd
5 Princes Street
London W1R 8PH

Levencrafts
54 Church Square
Guisborough, Yorkshire

John Lewis and Co Ltd
Oxford Street
London W1

Sesame Ventures
Greenham Hall
Wellington, Somerset

Leather

The Light Leather Company
16 Soho Square
London W1

Gloving leather

Milners
67 Queen Street
Hitchin, Hertfordshire

Suede and leather offcuts

Redpath Campbell and Partners Ltd
Department CH13
Cheapside
Stroud, Gloucestershire

Vilene and Bondaweb

Dressmakers' suppliers

Foam

Woolworth branches
Upholsterers' suppliers
Market stalls

Clear resin kits

Bondaglass Ltd
158 Ravenscroft Road
Beckenham, Kent

Griffin and George
Ealing Road
Alperton, Wembley
Middlesex

Marvin medium

Margros Ltd
Monument House
Monument Way West
Woking, Surrey

Berol Ltd
Oldmeadow Road
Kings' Lynn, Norfolk

Copydex, Polycell, dowel rods

Do It Yourself shops
Model shops

Perspex, rota cane

Dryad Ltd
Northgates
Leicester

Invicta Plastic Ltd
Oadby, Leicester

Parbond

Craft shops

Protasil

Carpet shops
Upholsterers' suppliers

Dartboard frames

Sports shops

**Foil, papers
coloured acetate**

Paperchase Products Ltd
216 Tottenham Court Road
London W1

Cinemoid
Rank Strand Electric
250 Kensington Lane
London SE11

Suppliers in the USA

Most of the materials can be bought from large department stores, craft shops or Do It Yourself shops

Embroidery threads and accessories, and fabrics

American Crewel and Canvas Studio
P O Box 298, Boonton
New Jersey 07005

Coats and Clark's Sales Corp
430 Park Avenue
New York, NY 10022
and branches at
Atlanta, Baltimore, Chicago, Cleveland,
Dallas, Los Angeles, Fairlawn, Portland
and St Louis

Craft Yarns
Main Street
Harrisville
Rhode Island and
230 Fifth Avenue
New York, NY 10001

F J Fawcett Inc
129 South Street
Boston
Massachusetts 02111

Lily Mills Co
Shelby
North Carolina 28150

The Needle's Point Studio
7013 Duncraig Court
McLean
Virginia 22101

The Thread Shed
307 Freeport Road
Pittsburgh
Pennsylvania 15215

Beads and sequins

Hollander Bead Corp
25 West 37 Street
New York, NY 10018

Walbead Inc
38 West 37 Street
New York, NY 10018

Marvin medium

Eagle Pencil Company
Danbury
Connecticut

Index

Figures in *italics* refer to illustrations

Appliqué 14, 36, 39, 68, 71, 75, 95, 96, 100, *17*
    leathers and suede 57, 58, 78

Bags 33, 96, *96*, *97*
Beads and sequins 14, 71, 75, 78, 90, 92, 94, 99, 102
Beads, glass 96
    gold 96
    wooden 76
Beads on leather 58
Beads, paper, to make 92, 93, *93*
    log, to make 93
Blackwork 76
Bostik, clear 78
Bugles 71, 92
Burses 112

Card 102, 110, 112
Cardboard cylinders 102
    rings 35
Cinemoid 15, 24, 78, 100, 102
Copydex (strong white glue) 9, 38, 92, 112
Curtain rings 30
Cut work 15, 73, *42*

Deliberate mistakes 50, 62, *52*
Dowel rods 100
Dress 46, *48*

Ecclesiastical embroidery 7, 43, 112
Embroidery without a background 22, *23*

Fabric, types of
    cheese cloth 44, *44*
    chiffon 102
    crêpe 108
    dralon 46
    even weave 46
    furnishing 35
    gauze 102
    loosely woven 42
    polythene sacks 75
    satin woven 46
    Scandinavian *41*
    semi-transparent 68
    twill 46, *49*
    tweedy furnishing 95
    woollen 107
Fabric, methods of treating
    burning 57
    cutting 57
    cut holes in 42
    manipulating threads 39

    tearing 57
    rumpling 57
    scorching 39
Finnish needleweaving 26, 35, *15*
Foam 95, 96, 112
    chopped 107
Frame, corner *16*
    hinged 13, *13*
    right angled double 13
Frames 8–22, *12*, *13*
    to cover 10, *10*, *11*
    to make 8
Frames, lampshade 26
    wire dartboard 24, *27*, *28*

Glass fronted box 22
Gold kid 96, 110

Hat 46, *47*
Holes 14, 15, *14*, *21*
    based on curtain rings 73, *73*

Inspiration from unusual objects 66–78
    acetate sheeting 77
    barrel tops 36, *36*
    ceramic tiles 75, *75*
    clear *bostick* 78
    cooking foil 68
    corks 68
    cylinders 75, 102
    dried vegetables 67
    drinking straws 66, 109
    egg boxes 68
    eyelets 71
    feathers 66, 67
    fish bones 66
    hardboard 77
    loofah 68
    marvin medium 78
    metal scraps 78
    nails, tin-tacks, screws 75
    orange peel 67
    oxtail bones 66
    paper 76
    pasta 68
    pegboard 76
    plastic tubing 71
    polythene sheeting 75
    rubber rings, washers 71
    spinal bones 66
    vacuum formed shapes 75
    wire 69
    wood shavings 76

Kapok 108

Lampshades 15, 34, 69, 71, 76, *29–32*, *34*
    decoration of 39
Leathers and suedes 57, 110

appliqué 78, *59, 60, 61*
  experiments with *58*
  manipulating 60
  padding 60
  punching 57

Manipulating fabrics 39–65, *40, 41*
Marvin medium 34, 38, 77, 78, 93, 110
Melinex (acetate) 30, 75, 77, 100

Needles 88
  chenille 88
Needleweaving 14, 24, 26, 46, 50, 56, 58, 100, *17, 42*
  chequerboard *49, 53*
  Finnish 26, *35*
  surface 81

Padding 94, 96, 107
Panama patchwork 99, *99*
Parbond 15, 100, 102, 112
Perspex, plexiglass 102, 110
Polycell 34, 76
Polyfilla 92, 93
Polythene bags 107
Pulpit fall 42, 112, *43*

Rota cane 73, *74*
Rubber rings 59, 60, 71, 96
  washers *74*

Sculptures 95–112
Semi-precious stones 78
Stitches
  back 88
  braid 90
  bullion knot 80
  buttonhole 69, 71, 80, 84, 96, *80, 83*
    knotted 80
    lacy 15, 30, 33, 68, 75, 77, 81, 108
  chain 81, 84, 90
    crested 80
    knotted 80
    piled *87*
    chained wheatear *80*
    chevron 81
    diagonal 81
    cobbler 81
    couching 71
    cretan 26, 68, 69, 80, 88
    darning 26
    double knot 80, 81
    double twisted lattice *81*
    feather 80, 88
    fishbone 79
    florentine 81
    fly 81
      knotted 80
    french knot 68, 80, 81, 84, 92, 102

guilloche 80, 81
hem 46, 50
herringbone 26, 68, 79, 81, 84, *79, 82*
honeycomb 81
interlacing 80
invisible 39, 77, 96
ladder 90
link 81
long 81
long armed double knot *80*
needlepoint lace 81
plait 81
raised chain band 90, *91*
raised stem 80
rope 80, 88
running 79, 88
satin 81, 84, 90
seeding 81, 84
sheaf 90
short 81
Smyrna cross 81
stem 81, 84, 88
surface darning 81
surfacing needleweaving 81
vandyke 90, *91*
wave 81
wheatear 80
whipping 15, 26, 50, 71, 73, 80, 102
Stitches, *Group 1* 79–81
  chained 80
  composite 80
  flat 79
  lace 81
  looped 80
  Group 2 81
    canvas 81
    drawn ground 81
  Group 3 81–84
    filling 81
    line or outline 81
    shading 81
  Group 4 84
    surface 84
Suffolk puff patchwork 68, 96, 99, *99*
Supports, unusual 24–38
  carboys 24
  chipboard 100
  demijohns 24
  furniture 38
  hair brushes 38
  hand mirrors 38
  hat boxes 38
  lampshades 26
  large glass bottles 24
  old bicycle wheels 38
  plastic lettuce shakers 36
  polystyrene 36
  wire dartboards 24
  wire spark guards 36

wooden barrel tops 36
Stiletto 73, 88, 112

Tassels 92, 94
Threads
  clear *bostick* 78
  cotton 92
  fishing line 14
  floss silk 88
  gold 96
  linen 92
  mercerised embroidery 69, 93
  metal 78
  nylon 14
  polythene 76, *86*
  rug wool 71, 100
  string 71, 107, *24*
  sylko perlé no. 5 90

textured 88
thick embroidery cotton 88, 96
thick chenille 71
waxed 94
weaving 110
Threads, free cutting of 56
Three-layer embroidery *54, 55, 56*

Victorian Peep Show 14
  method 14
Vilene Bondaweb 34
Vilene, iron-on 10, 14, 33, 75, 94, 100, *21*

Window embroidery 22, *22*
Wire 68, 71, 92, 96, 102
  coat hangers 100
  copper 110
  netting 71